# Bible Names of Christ

*80 Names and Titles of Our Lord*

**Ivor Powell**

## BY THE SAME AUTHOR

*Bible Cameos*
*Bible Gems*
*Bible Highways*
*Bible Pinnacles*
*Bible Treasures*
*Bible Windows*
*David: His Life and Times*
*Matthew's Majestic Gospel*
*Mark's Superb Gospel*
*Luke's Thrilling Gospel*
*John's Wonderful Gospel*
*The Amazing Acts*
*The Exciting Epistle to the Ephesians*
*What in the World Will Happen Next?*

KREGEL PUBLICATIONS
Grand Rapids, Michigan 49501

Cover Design: Don Ellens
Cover Photo: David Malefyt

**Library of Congress Cataloging-in-Publication Data**

Powell, Ivor, 1910-
Bible Names of Christ.

Includes index.
1. Jesus Christ–Name–Meditations. I. Title.
BT590.N2P69 1988 232 87-29722

ISBN 0-8254-3530-7

2 3 4 5 6 Printing/Year 95 94 93 92 91 90

*Printed in the United States of America*

# CONTENTS

# PREFACE

Over a half century ago, I became fascinated with the many titles given to the Savior. The Scriptures were filled with names which glistened as facets of a diamond. They were all different, and each beautiful in its own setting. At that time my first book had been published, and I believed another volume, explaining the names of Jesus, would be helpful to all pastors. I began making a list of the names and titles of the Lord, and soon had eighty-three. It seemed I was well on my way to writing the desired book.

Then, my life and ministry were dramatically changed. I was invited to become the national evangelist of my church in South Africa, and that request was followed by others from Australia, New Zealand, Canada, and California. During the succeeding years I preached around the world, and, slowly, my Bible books made their appearance. The commentaries on the four Gospels and the Acts of the Apostles followed, but after many years of writing and preaching the gospel, I had grown weary.

I shall never forget the day when my last commentary was completed. I put down my pen, and breathing a sigh of relief, said, "Thank you , Lord; I have finished." Then, suddenly, a voice whispered, "What about the names of the Savior?" Frankly, I was astounded, for that project of my youth had been completely forgotten. The thought had not even occurred to me in decades.

Eventually, I began making a new list of the Lord's names, and during my evangelistic crusades in the eastern states of America, I borrowed typewriters and, in the motels where I stayed, began to write this book. The task has now been completed, and with a prayer for its blessing, I send the volume on its mission. May it bring blessing to all who preach the glorious gospel of the grace of God.

Once again I am indebted to my wife, Betty, whose careful and skillful editing of my studies polished the facets of this diamond. Let me add that I enjoyed writing this book more than I did any of its predecessors. When describing the various themes of the Bible, it was necessary to mention various scenes and expound many doctrines. This book has one theme—The Lord Jesus Christ. Long ago, strangers went to Philip to say, "Sir, we would see Jesus." If such people came to me today, I would give them a copy of this book.

IVOR POWELL

Santa Barbara, California

# THE SEED OF THE WOMAN

(Genesis 3:15)

The title or definition "The Seed of the Woman" was the first reference made in the Scriptures to the Messiah. It was and ever will remain intriguing because it was spoken by God in the presence of Adam and Eve, who could not have understood what was being uttered. Yet it made such an impression upon their minds that they never forgot what was said. They repeated it to their children, who passed it on to their descendents. Ultimately, when the Book of Genesis was written, the author was able to repeat what God uttered centuries earlier. If for no other reason, the text becomes one of the most fascinating in the Bible.

*The strange message (Gen. 3:14-15)*

"And the Lord God said unto the serpent, Because thou hast done this, thou art cursed above all cattle. . . . And I will put enmity between thee and the woman, and between thy seed and her seed; it shall bruise thy head, and thou shalt bruise his heel." It should be remembered that the methods of childbirth at that time had not been explored; no child had ever been born. Adam and his wife had only just commenced exploring the wonderful possibilities of living. After many centuries of scientific and medical research, much has become known about the miracle of procreation, and gynecologists are able to offer expert help to expectant mothers. No such knowledge or help was available in the Garden of Eden. There were neither hospitals nor doctors, and the cry of a new-born infant had yet to be heard. To speak of *the seed of the woman* could not have conveyed enlightenment to the man and woman who heard the original statement.

*The sublime miracle (Matt. 1:23)*

"Behold, a virgin shall be with child, and shall bring forth a son, and they shall call his name Emmanuel, which being interpreted is, God with us." Today doctors speak about artificial insemination, when the sperm of a male is inserted into a woman to make bearing a child possible. This system was not known in Bible days, and therefore it was completely impossible—without a miracle from God—for a virgin to become pregnant. To be absolutely sure of my facts, I asked one of my doctor-friends to explain, and perhaps corroborate, what I already knew. He answered by speaking of the intact hymen, or veil, which extends over the female vaginal orifice and said this was not broken except by the intrusion of the male organ when sperm was transmitted to fertilize the egg produced by the female. The child thus produced became a combination of two natures, and resemblance to the producing parents may often be seen in the features of the offspring.

*The sinless Master (Heb. 4:15)*

The birth of Jesus was different! Mary's hymen was broken *from the inside.* She was truly a virgin since she had not had intercourse with Joseph, the man to whom she was betrothed. Since the fall of Adam and Eve, all people are born sinners. Sin is a nature transmitted from generation to generation, and unfortunately, as David suggested, we are born in sin, and "shapen in iniquity" (see Psalm 51:5). However much critical people may argue to the contrary, Mary was a sinner, born of sinful parents who came from sinful generations of ancestors. Had Jesus received a corrupt nature *either from Joseph or Mary,* He would have been born a sinner and would have needed a redeemer. The Spirit of God "hovered" over Mary and did within her what needed to be done. That baby was *born of God, not humans.* From the creation of the fetus, through its development and until the Child was born, the entire operation was controlled by the Holy Spirit. But that suggests an important question. If Jesus were all of God, how could He be human? *That* is the miracle of the Incarnation. At some point, Jesus embraced humanity—not fallen humanity, but the type which was evident in Adam before he sinned. Thereafter, the humanity and divinity of Christ were so inextricably woven together that it was almost impossible to tell them apart. Mary, the chosen woman through whom the Son of God came to earth, was greatly privileged. She will be associated eternally with the Redeemer, for even from the beginning of time, her Child was known as *the seed of the woman.* Paul wrote of that wonderful Baby: "Great is the mystery of godliness: God was manifest in the flesh, justified in the Spirit, seen of angels, preached unto the Gentiles, believed on in the world, received up into glory (1 Tim. 3:16).

> Jesus, Oh, how sweet the Name
> Jesus, every day the same.
> Jesus, let all saints proclaim,
> His worthy praise forever.

# I AM THAT I AM

(EXODUS 3:14; JOHN 18:5-6)

The most profound and awe-inspiring name ever given to God was given by Him. Long before the universe existed, God planned its creation. When neither angelic nor human eyes could behold, God moved with indescribable majesty to say, "Let there be," ...and there was. Whence He came, how He operated and what were the inexhaustible attributes of His transcendent glory are revelations beyond human understanding. He always was, and ever will be, the infinite God. Men were taught to call Him "Heavenly Father;" angels recognized Him as the inspired Creator, but when Jehovah spoke of Himself, He said, "I AM THAT I AM."

*The I AM of authentic purpose*

Moses was exceedingly apprehensive concerning his future. God had commissioned him to deliver the captive nation in Egypt, but the job was frightening. When he told God of his inability to be an eloquent speaker, he was informed that Aaron would be the spokesman in the court of Egypt. Becoming somewhat desperate, Moses used a different argument, reminding God of the stubbornness of Israel and of the certainty of their asking for his credentials. He asked, "Whom shall I say sent me?" God replied with the Name above every name. "And God said unto Moses, I AM THAT I AM: and he said, Thus shalt thou say unto the children of Israel, *I AM* hath sent me unto you...this is my name forever, and this is my memorial unto all generations" (Exod. 3:14-15).

*The I AM of amazing power*

Probably, one of the most sensational events seen during the life and ministry of Jesus took place in the Garden of Gethsemane, where Jehovah's name disarmed the multitude which came to arrest the Savior. "Jesus...went forth, and said unto them, Whom seek ye? They answered him, Jesus of Nazareth. Jesus saith unto them, *I am*...As soon then as he had said unto them, *I am,* they went backward, and fell to the ground" (John 18:4-6). The explanation of that miraculous event is very simple. Jesus was God, and that was one of the occasions when His humanity failed to hide the inherent glory of the Godhead. When He said, "I AM," He released immeasurable power that could have slain an army. Demoralized, frightened, and helpless, the soldiers fell to the ground, and it was only when Christ's power was withdrawn that they rose to their feet and bound their Prisoner. He was God; His name was God's name; but, unfortunately, the men were too blind to see the significance of that hallowed moment.

*The I AM of assured provision*

God found and delivered His people in Egypt and led them on their journey to the Promised Land. He wished them to know, and remember, that their Redeemer would never leave them. The Lord Jesus Christ taught identical truth. Almost every day He used the same formula I AM but in many delightful ways added words to indicate the extent of His care. He said, "I am *the Bread, the Way, the Door, the Truth, the Life, the Light, the Good Shepherd, the Resurrection."* John, who began his Gospel with an affirmation of the deity of his Lord, apparently enjoyed expounding the boundless treasure enshrined within the eternal Name.

Paul evidently comprehended, at least to a small degree, the limitless wonder of this inscrutable truth. He wrote to Timothy, saying: "Now unto the King eternal, immortal, invisible, the only wise God, be honor and glory forever and ever. Amen" (1 Tim. 1:17).

# THE HEALER

(EXODUS 15:26; PSALM 103:3; LUKE 4:18-19)

Although the writers of the New Testament never gave this name to the Lord, it may be assumed that He was so called by most of the inhabitants of Palestine. When Christ spoke to the disciples of John the Baptist, He said, "Tell John what things ye have seen and heard; how that the blind see, the lame walk, the lepers are cleansed, the deaf hear, the dead are raised . . ." (Luke 7:22). God made a special promise to Israel. "If thou wilt diligently hearken unto the voice of the LORD, thy God. . .I will put none of these diseases upon you which I have brought upon the Egyptians: for *I am the LORD that healeth thee*" (Exod. 15:26). His promise was conditional. God said healing would depend on Israel's obedience to Jehovah. When Christ ministered in Palestine, the Jews had violated the commands of the Almighty and forfeited their right to blessing. It became apparent that the formula for healing had changed. Jesus said: "If *thou canst believe,* all things are possible to him that believeth" (Mark 9:23).

*Christ healed the sick. . .His glorious power*

"Now when the sun was setting, all they that had any sick with diverse diseases brought them unto him; and he laid his hands on every one of them, and healed them" (Luke 4:40). The verse describes what may have been the most resplendent scene in the Bible. It was eventide when anxious people brought their sick to Jesus. Gently, the Lord touched every sick person, and the result was amazing. The sun was setting, but another Sun was rising with healing in His wings (see Mal. 4:2). There was no shouting—unless it came from grateful suppliants; there were no theatrical displays. The Lord gently placed His hand on the upturned faces of needy people, and they were healed. Language cannot describe the wonder of those hallowed moments. Heaven came down to earth, and the glory of the Infinite became apparent. God continues to heal men and women, but no faith-healer has ever been able to emulate the deeds of the Savior. Jesus never failed to heal any penitent sinner. His work was permanent; the people did not go home to suffer a relapse within a few weeks.

*Christ healed consciences. . .His gracious purpose*

Sometimes the scars on a man's conscience may be more devastating than the wounds in his body. The continuing pain from a guilty conscience may be more distressing than any infirmity. Physical healing may be an assured fact, but when a person's former indiscretions continue to haunt, memories become death-blows. Perhaps the Lord had this in mind when He said to the adulteress:

"Neither do I condemn thee: go, and sin no more" (John 8:11). It is thrilling to remember the words spoken by God through Jeremiah the prophet. "I will forgive their iniquity, and *I will remember their sin no more*" (Jer. 31:34). Evidently, the Lord desired the woman to concentrate more on future endeavor than to dwell on past failure. Occasionally, a person accepts forgiveness from God, but has difficulty forgiving himself! The Lord not only forgave, He forgot! Since God has cast our sins "into the depths of the sea" (Micah 7:19), we should be content to leave them there. Many people try to salvage what God has buried; they like to remain miserable!

*Christ healed families . . . His great pleasure*

It will always be interesting to remember that Paul was not the first member of his family to become a Christian. Writing to the Roman church, the apostle said: "Salute Andronicus and Junia, my kinsmen, and my fellowprisoners, who are of note among the apostles, *who also were in Christ before me*" (Rom. 16:7). There has been much discussion concerning the identity of these "kinsmen," but it is known that Paul had a sister who lived in Jerusalem (see Acts 23:16). If she were named Junia, she must have been distressed when her brother persecuted the Christians. Doubtless, her prayers were answered when Saul yielded himself to the Lord. Christ solved problems within families. The promise: "I am the LORD that healeth thee" (Exod. 15:26), reached every area of life; it was never difficult to understand why Christ was known as the Healer of men and women. Believing prayer offered in His name can accomplish anything.

# A PROPHET

(DEUTERONOMY 18:15-22; JOHN 4:19)

Prophets were among the most important people in Israel. Their ministry was two-fold. They told-forth the message of God; that is, they were preachers who witnessed regarding the advisability of observing the Mosaic law. Secondly, they were inspired men to whom God imparted knowledge of future events. There were false prophets, who preached to please their audience and lived on the offerings given by deluded listeners. A notable example of this type is found in 1 Kings 22:7-8, where, after a compromising speech made by four hundred prophets, Jehoshaphat, the king of Judah, asked: "Is there not here a prophet of the Lord besides, that we may inquire of him? And the king of Israel said unto Jehoshaphat, There is yet one man, Micaiah, the son of Imlah, by whom we may inquire of the Lord: but I hate him; for he doth not prophesy good concerning me, but evil." In the light of that scripture, it was easy to understand why God said to Moses: "When a prophet speaketh in the name of the Lord, *if the thing follow not, nor come to pass,* that is the thing which the Lord hath not spoken, but the prophet hath spoken it presumptuously: thou shalt not be afraid of him" (Deut. 18:22). Moses, aware of this situation, described how God said: "I will raise them up a Prophet from among their brethren, like unto thee, and will put my words in his mouth; and he shall speak unto them all that I shall command him" (Deut. 18:18).

*A true prophet is divinely commissioned*

This fact is indisputable. No one but God can anoint a preacher with supernatural power. A theological college may train candidates for the ministry; an attentive student may improve his skills and become an outstanding orator, but the power of the Holy Spirit, the dynamic that changes lives, is something which only God can give. He who represents God must be acquainted with Him; the minister who would communicate truth to a congregation must first be an excellent listener! His study should be an upper room, and not a lounge! When the Samaritan woman looked into the face of Jesus, she became aware that, in some strange but delightful fashion, He was different!

*A true prophet is definitely committed*

Having received instructions from God, he proceeds on his special assignment, determined to perform his God-given task. This becomes the deepest conviction in his soul and the driving force behind his ministry. Throughout the ministry of the Savior, His listeners became increasingly aware that this determination was evident in everything He said and did. It would be impossible to find an occasion when the Lord did anything for Himself. His only desire was to heal broken hearts and bodies. When Jesus became tired, He slept; when He was hungry, He ate. But even meeting His personal needs was done that He might be strengthened to make His ministry more effective.

*A true prophet is decidely conscientious*

Even prophets are human, and there were times when some turned their faces away from God. Their confidence was undermined, and they became unworthy of their calling. Jonah and Elijah both failed in this respect. Yet, when those men remembered the place from which they had fallen, their repentance led to a renewal of confidence in Jehovah. *No prophet ever failed when he continued to look into the face of God.* Christ's fellowship with the Father remained unbroken, until He bore our sins to the cross. It was only then that, temporarily, sin interfered with His happiness. Jesus lived, moved, and had His being in the center of the divine will. He was completely conscientious toward God and men.

*A true prophet is deliberately communicative*

The Bible describes incidents when men of lesser stature "hid their light under a bushel." Fear of unpleasant repercussions from an antagonistic audience ruined their courage; their message was never delivered. There were occasions when compromising orators endeavored to please listeners, and the effectiveness of their words was ruined. Jesus was completely different. He spoke as the Oracle of God, and intelligent hearers gave attention to everything He uttered. The Samaritan woman listened to *His witness* and said, "I perceive that thou art a prophet" (John 4:19). The blind beggar beheld *His works* and came to the same conclusion (John 9:17). Throughout the history of the Church, all wise people who have considered the message of the Savior, inevitably said, "That a great prophet is risen up among us; and, that God hath visited his people" (Luke 7:16). "Hear ye him" (see Matt. 17:5).

# THE CAPTAIN OF SALVATION

(JOSHUA 5:13-14; HEBREWS 2:10)

The term *captain* does not mean today what it did in Bible times. A captain is now a soldier of rank, superior to privates, corporals, and sergeants, but inferior to colonels, generals, and supreme commanders. Throughout the Old Testament era, a captain held the highest military honor, and each person appointed to that illustrious position was responsible for the welfare of the nation. To him, the tribes looked for guidance and protection. He was subservient only to the king; his word was law; his decisions were final; his courage and influence was recognized by every person in Israel. When the Lord was called the Captain of our salvation, the Church recognized the risen Savior to be the anointed representative of the King Eternal.

*This Captain controls . . . He is present*

Probably, the greatest illustration of God's powerful presence is found in Joshua 5:13-15. When Israel's leader was about to attack the city of Jericho, "There stood a man over against him with his sword drawn in his hand: and Joshua went unto him and said unto him, Art thou for us, or for our adversaries? And he said, Nay: but as captain of the host of the Lord am I now come. And Joshua fell on his face to the earth, and did worship, and said unto him, What saith my Lord unto his servant? And the captain of the Lord's host said unto Joshua, Loose thy shoe from off thy foot; for the place whereon thou standest is holy. And Joshua did so." The Captain of the Lord's host was not seen again, but Joshua remained assured He was never far away. The ceremony of removing a shoe from a foot had great significance in Israel. If a man were unable to perform certain acts, he confessed this by the removal of a shoe (see Deut. 25:5-10; Ruth 4:7-8). When Joshua observed this rite, he confessed his inability to lead Israel into Canaan and gladly allowed the Captain to assume control of his army.

*This Captain commands . . . He is preeminent*

Within any nation it would be unthinkable and inexcusable to oppose the edict of a supreme commander. The man who leads the nation's armed forces would have been trained for his position and considered capable of overcoming any danger. When God appointed the Lord Jesus to become the Leader of heaven's forces, He exhibited complete confidence in the ability of the Savior to do whatever became necessary in the conflict against evil. Emulating the example set by Joshua, the Church should recognize her inadequacy to overcome evil. The soldiers of the Lord should "take off their shoes'' and confess sincerely that they are completely dependent on the unseen Commander.

*This Captain commends . . . He is perceptive*

Sometimes, during a conflict, the supreme commander of an army may honor soldiers for meritorious conduct under fire. In the presence of assembled officers and men, he may pin a medal on the uniform of a hero. This is true of the Lord Jesus Christ; He is always aware of the faithfulness of His soldiers. Speaking to His first followers, He explained that not even a cup of water given in His name would be unrewarded; every deed done to extend His kingdom, whether great or small, would be rewarded with ''good measure, pressed down, and shaken together, and running over'' (see Luke 6:38). Yet, by the same standard, Christ also might condemn those whose cowardice became apparent.

*This Captain conquers . . . He is praiseworthy*

''And I beheld, and I heard the voice of many angels round about the throne and the beasts and the elders: and the number of them was ten thousand times ten thousand, and thousands of thousands; saying with a loud voice, Worthy is the Lamb that was slain'' (Rev. 5:11-12). Christians may appear to lose occasional battles, but their ultimate victory is assured. The Hamans, Neros, and Hitlers appeared to be invincible, but they perished. The battle cry of God's people should always be, ''If God be for us, who can be against us?''

# THE REDEEMER

(Job 19:25)

It is interesting to discover that in at least eighteen places in the Old Testament, God is said to be the Redeemer of His people. A careful consideration of these scriptures reveal God as the Redeemer of the nation and of the individual in a suggestive progression of thought. Jeremiah said, "*Their* Redeemer is strong; the LORD of hosts is his name: he shall thoroughly plead their cause, that he may give rest to the land, and disquiet the inhabitants of Babylon" (Jer. 50:34). Isaiah appeared to be more personal when he prayed and said, "Thou, O Lord, art our father, *our* redeemer; thy name is from everlasting" (Isa. 63:16). Job went even further in his testimony. He said, "For I know that *my* redeemer liveth, and that he shall stand at the latter day upon the earth" (Job 19:25). Explaining the word *redemption,* the *Reader's Digest Encyclopedic Dictionary* says it means, "to regain possession by paying a price." The Greek word which is translated "redeemer," or "redemption" is *lutrees,* which means "to pay a price—*to cause to be released to one's self.*" This signified that whatever was redeemed became the property of the redeemer. When a man was redeemed, he became the slave of the master who redeemed him. That truth, when applied to the theology of the New Testament, becomes exceedingly interesting.

*The discernment of a sufferer*

It was significant that when overwhelmed by sorrow, Job did not refer to Jehovah as the Almighty, but as his Redeemer. There were certain unalterable laws which governed redemption. Any benefactor could help, cheer, or advise a slave, but only a member of his family could redeem him (see Lev. 25:47-49). In order for God to redeem sinners, He had to become human; "to become bone of their bone, and flesh of their flesh" (see Gen. 2:23). Therefore, He brought about the miracle of the Incarnation when the Word was made flesh and dwelt among us. The prophets frequently referred to God as the Redeemer of Israel, for He had delivered His people from the slavery of Egypt. When Christ came to earth, He came to accomplish a redemption hitherto unknown.

*The deliverance of a slave*

Apparently Job was aware of a greater slavery than the physical problems which had ruined his health. He recognized himself to be a sinner needing eternal redemption. When he said, "I know that my redeemer liveth, and that he shall stand at the latter day upon the earth," he spoke with the authority and vision of a prophet. Job was aware of his physical condition and foresaw the time when his body would be completely destroyed. The words "though... worms destroy this body," suggest he had no illusions about his future. Yet, nothing could destroy his faith that in spite of everything, *"in his flesh,* he would see God." To make this possible, he would need to have a new body and to be raised triumphantly from the grave. If we may use the words of Paul, Job was one "born out of due time." He was a New Testament saint who lived in an Old Testament age!

*The delight of the soul*

"Whom I shall see for myself, and mine eyes shall behold, and not another" (Job 19:27). It was almost inconceivable that, in spite of his unprecedented anguish, perfect peace flooded the soul of the patriarch. Although his body was covered with boils and pain was unceasing, Job said, "But he knoweth the way that I take: when he hath tried me, I shall come forth as gold" (Job 23:10). Engulfed in the darkness of his experiences, the saint saw a bright and shining light, the harbinger of a new day. A Redeemer who cared so much for slaves could not be indifferent to his misery. When Job grasped these sublime truths, his life was completely transformed. He was able to sing in the dark!

I know that my Redeemer liveth,
And on the earth, again shall stand.
I know eternal life He giveth,
That grace and power are in His hand.
I know, I know that Jesus liveth,
And on the earth again shall stand.

# THE ROSE OF SHARON; AND THE LILY OF THE VALLEY

(SONG OF SOLOMON 2:1)

The rose and the lily have always been attributed to Christ, although within the Bible He was never so called. Christians associated the beauty of the flowers with Him who is called "the fairest among ten thousand" and the "altogether lovely One" (Song of Sol. 5:10,16). Abishag, a young woman in Israel, was requested to become David's companion during the closing days of his life (1 Kings 1:1-4). Among the gifts she received was a beautiful home in a picturesque garden. Some theologians believe that the Song of Solomon reflected the love of Solomon for a desired bride. Others see a forgotten shepherd who went in search of his sweetheart. They teach that the girl was entangled in a web of her own weaving; she was attracted to the shepherd but fascinated by a doting monarch. The identity of the lover is not essential to the understanding of the text. The would-be bridegroom, whoever he might have been, said: "I am the rose of Sharon, and the lily of the valleys" (Song of Sol. 2:1).

*The perfume of the blossoms*

The flowers mentioned in the text have no relationship with modern plants bearing the same names. (1) Some expositors . . . understand the beautiful white-scented narcissus, common in the spring in the plains of Sharon, to be the flower mentioned. (2) A Syriac word suggests the colchicum or crocus, which are strikingly alike, and which, when the rainy season begins, carpet the fields with bright flowers. (3) Tristram (a noted author), however, judges that the oleander is meant from its growing at Jericho, and by the waters, in these passages (*Dictionary of the Bible,* J. D. Davis, pp. 600-661). The only conclusion resulting from the continuing discussions is that both the rose of Sharon, and the lily of the valleys, were flowers of entrancing beauty. This explains why the twin names have always been associated with Christ.

*The person of the bridegroom*

When Paul wrote to the Philippians, he used very interesting language: "But I have all, and abound; I am full, having received of Epaphroditus the things which were sent from you, *an odor of a sweet smell,* a sacrifice acceptable, wellpleasing to God" (Phil. 4:18). Ezra spoke of "sacrifices of sweet savors unto the God of heaven" (Ezra 6:10), and Moses often mentioned sacrifices from which sweet odors ascended to Jehovah. It is evident that certain details of the worship of Israel pleased God. Was this expressed when Jesus said, "For I do always those things that please him"? (John 8:29). The words and actions of Christ resembled rare and beautiful flowers in God's garden; their fragrance enthralled the Divine Gardener. The bridegroom, as seen in the Song of Solomon, was a type of the greatest of all bridegrooms—the head and husband of the Church. It must have been wonderful to walk with Jesus and to listen to the words He uttered. Unfortunately, we can only look back through the centuries and speculate about His appearance. The poet was correct when he wrote:

> Fair is the sunshine
> Fairer still the moonlight
> And all the twinkling starry host.
> Jesus shines brighter;
> Jesus shines purer,
> Than all the angels heaven can boast.

*The privilege of the bride*

God the Father gazed with infinite satisfaction upon the Lord Jesus; everything He saw was extremely wonderful. The perfume which emanated from the righteousness of Christ never diminished. Jesus was a continuing delight to God the Father and the heavenly hosts; He was adorned with fadeless beauty and possessed all the loveliness known in time and eternity. The Lord was truly the Rose of Sharon and the Lily of the valleys. When we reflect on the Song of Solomon, it is unbelievable to us that such a glorious man should seek the love of an ordinary woman. Similarly, it seems beyond understanding why the Prince of Heaven should seek the love and fellowship of sinners. It has always been difficult to understand the intricacies of love, but when men try to fathom Christ's love for sinners, they attempt the impossible. We can only exclaim with Norman J. Clayton:

> Now I belong to Jesus;
> Jesus belongs to me
> Not for the years of time alone,
> But for eternity.

# WONDERFUL

(ISAIAH 9:6; JUDGES 13:18)

Isaiah 9:6 is one of the most important verses in the Old Testament writings. Speaking concerning the expected Messiah, the prophet uttered details which will engage the attention of scholars until the end of time. The magnitude and importance of his declaration beggars description, for his quintuplet of names present truth beyond comprehension. Isaiah wrote: "For unto us a child is born, unto us a son is given: and the government shall be upon his shoulder: and his name shall be called, *Wonderful, Counsellor, the mighty God, the everlasting Father, the Prince of Peace.*" All these names deserve special consideration.

*Wonderful in His person*

The *Reader's Digest Encyclopedic Dictionary* says that the word *wonderful* means "of such a nature as to excite wonder, or marvelous." The same source says that the word *marvelous,* means, "*causing astonishment; amazing; extraordinary; miraculous; incredible.*" Isaiah desired his readers to understand that all these characteristics would be seen in the Messiah. There is a remarkable story in the thirteenth chapter of the Book of Judges which describes how an angel appeared to Manoah and his wife. God's messenger announced the promise of a son to the childless couple. When they asked for the angel's name, he replied: "Why askest thou thus after my name, seeing it is *secret?*" The marginal rendering explains the word translated *secret* means "wonderful!" Many theologians believe this was one of the theophanies, that is, one of the appearances of God in human form occasionally mentioned in the Old Testament (compare Heb. 7:2-3).

*Wonderful in His preaching (John 7:46)*

John described in his Gospel how the chief priests and Pharisees sent officers to arrest Jesus, but the officials paused to listen as the Savior preached to His audience. They became increasingly nonplussed and, when they returned, could only exclaim, "Never man spake like this man." They listened as words of grace came from the Lord's lips. Doubtless, they had often arrested an offender, but Jesus was different. His presence suggested that God was close at hand, and yet in some indefinable way, He was the most precious friend any man could know. The Lord was a Person of surpassing excellence, and to lay arresting hands on Him appeared to be beyond reason. It is easy to sympathize with those troubled officials. Modern readers are thrilled by reading what Jesus said, but to have been attending His meetings, looking into His face, and hearing every word of His message were experiences which exceeded anything they had known. Jesus was indeed wonderful!

*Wonderful in His power (Luke 5:26)*

John, who wrote about his Master, described many events which took place during the ministry of the Lord, but, finally, he concluded his manuscript by writing, "And there are also many other things which Jesus did, the which, if they should be written every one, I suppose that even the world itself could not contain the books that should be written" (John 21:25). Luke mentions one of the events which John omitted, the healing of the man who was brought to Christ by his four friends. What was heard and seen on that memorable occasion was clearly indicated by the reactions of the people who said, "We have seen strange things today." Even they admitted that Jesus was different from all other preachers.

*Wonderful in His purpose (Eph. 2:15-16)*

Paul was probably the greatest exponent of the truth expressed in the following statement about Christ: ". . . to make in himself of twain one new man, so making peace; and that he might reconcile both [Jews and Gentiles] unto God in one body by the cross, having slain the enmity thereby." The Savior planned to destroy the animosity between nations, and to create a new system in which all people would become unified in Him. Happiness would replace bitterness, fellowship would outlaw racial prejudice. To make this possible, He sacrificed Himself for sinners and created an atmosphere in which gratitude banished hatred. There was no other person who could accomplish this miracle, and therefore we exclaim that Jesus was the most wonderful man who ever walked on earth. Isaiah was inspired when he said, "His name shall be called *Wonderful.*"

# COUNSELOR

(ISAIAH 9:6)

The term "counselor" may be defined in two ways. It can mean *one who offers advice* and in this connection refers to a marriage counselor or an experienced man or woman who offers advice in camps, schools, or other institutions. The term may also be used to describe attorneys who either defend or prosecute an accused person. British people refer to them as barristers, professional men and women who "argue cases in the courts" (*Reader's Digest Encyclopedic Dictionary*). It would be interesting to know which of these ideas was in the mind of the prophet when he wrote his immortal text. The possibility exists that he was thinking of both.

*The cautious Counselor (Matt. 22:15-22)*

When the Herodians came to question the Savior, they said, "Tell us therefore. . .is it lawful to give tribute unto Caesar, or not?" The Lord replied, "Why tempt ye me, ye hypocrites? Shew me the tribute money. And they brought unto him a penny. And he saith unto them, Whose is this image and superscription? They say unto him, Caesar's. Then saith he unto them, Render therefore unto Caesar the things which are Caesar's; and unto God the things that are God's. When they heard these words, they marvelled, and left him, and went their way." Jesus was always cautious when He was asked to give advice. Someone has since said, "Fools rush in where angels fear to tread." That was never seen in the actions of the Lord. He was careful in assessing the merits of a case, and although His enemies tried repeatedly to lead Him into error, they failed. He never made a mistake, and His actions suggested a more efficient counselor could never be found.

*The confident Counselor (John 8:1-9)*

John described how, early one morning, when Jesus was teaching in the temple, the scribes and Pharisees brought to him a woman who had been arrested in the act of committing adultery. They said unto Him: "Master, this woman was taken in adultery, in the very act. Now Moses in the law commanded us, that such should be stoned: but what sayest thou?" These critics of the Lord were not seeking counsel, but trying to entangle Him in His statements so that they could bring serious charges against Him. The Savior looked at them, listened to their accusations, and then, as though He had heard nothing, stooped to write in the dust. What He ultimately said is known throughout the world. He demonstrated again that He was the best of all counselors, for He was not coerced into making rash statements; He was not stampeded into actions which afterward might have been regretted. What He said and did completely thwarted the plans made against Him, and when eventually He said, "He that is without sin among you, let him first cast a stone at her," the accusers were glad to escape out of His presence. Unwittingly, the unfortunate woman had found an excellent attorney who knew precisely what needed to be done. Her case was safe in His capable hands.

*The complete Counselor (Heb. 7:25)*

Comparing the Savior with the priests who had ministered in the temple, the writer to the Hebrews writes: "And they truly were many priests, because they were not suffered to continue by reason of death: but this man, because he continueth ever, hath an unchangeable priesthood. Wherefore, he is able also to save them to the uttermost that come unto God by him, *seeing he ever liveth to make intercession for them*" (Heb. 7:23-25).

When the Old Testament high priest entered into the presence of God, he wore on his chest a breastplate on which were written the names of the tribes of Israel. He stood at the mercy seat as the representative of all who placed their trust in him. Likewise, when the Lord Jesus Christ became our High Priest, He entered into the presence of God to make intercession for us. The poet expressed that glorious truth when he wrote:

> My name from the palms of His hands;
> Eternity cannot erase.
> More happy, but not more secure
> The glorified spirits in Heaven.

Christ is our legal counselor in the highest court in the universe. He never charges for His services; He never refuses to accept a client. It is stimulating to know He has never lost a case! "His name shall be called . . . Counselor."

# THE MIGHTY GOD

(ISAIAH 9:6)

During the lifetime of Isaiah, Israel and the adjacent nations believed in many types of man-made gods. Idolatry was a menace, and, unfortunately, many of the chosen race were susceptible to false religions. No man seemed to care that the gods were motionless and useless. The idols could move neither hand nor foot; they neither heard nor spoke. The prophet surely sighed with satisfaction when he spoke of the coming Messiah. Unlike the powerless gods of the nations, the expected One would be *the Mighty God;* all who saw Him would see Jehovah *in action.*

*The sublimity of the name*

It is interesting to know that, in the Old Testament, there are at least 213 texts where the gods of the nations are mentioned. There are other verses where the word *idols* is substituted for *gods.* Yet, never on any occasion is an idol, or god, referred to as *the Mighty God.* First Samuel 4:7-8 describes the fear of the Philistines when they heard shouting emanating from the camp of the Israelites. "And the Philistines were afraid, for they said, God is come into the camp. And they said, Woe unto us. . . .who shall deliver us out of the hand of *these mighty gods?* These are the gods that smote the Egyptians with all the plagues in the wilderness." The Philistines were heathens who, in their superstitious belief, attributed the miracles performed by Moses to mighty gods of whom they had little if any knowledge. No prophet ever said an idol was "mighty." That definition was reserved exclusively for Jehovah.

*The suggestiveness of the name*

When Isaiah predicted that the name of the Messiah would be *the Mighty God,* he implied that Jehovah would come to earth and that all His attributes would be seen in the expected Deliverer. This fact becomes fascinating when we consider that the strength of Jehovah was expressed in three ways: (1) *His Greatness in Creative Power.* Jeremiah said, "Ah, Lord God. . . .thou hast made the heaven and the earth by thy great power and stretched-out arm . . . the Great, *the Mighty God,* the Lord of Hosts, is his name" (Jer. 32:17-19). (2) *His Greatness in Selective Grace.* "Thus saith the Lord that made thee, and formed thee from the womb. . . Fear not, O Jacob, my servant; and thou, Jesurun, *whom I have chosen"* (Isa. 44:2). (3) *His Greatness in Compassionate Mercy.* "The Lord thy God in the midst of thee is *mighty;* he will save, he will rejoice over thee with joy" (Zeph. 3:17). Throughout the history of the Hebrew race, *the Mighty God* had manifested Himself in these ways. If the Messiah were to manifest identical characteristics, they would become visible in His ministry. Jesus "upheld all things by the word of his power" (Heb. 1:3). The Savior selected us before the foundation of the world (Eph. 1:4). Paul, writing to the Ephesian Christians, mentioned a love beyond dimension. "But God, who is rich in mercy, for his great love wherewith he loved us . . . hath quickened us together with Christ. . . ." (Eph. 2:4-5). God was to be in Christ, reconciling the world to Himself (2 Cor. 5:19), and that was one of the reasons why Isaiah said, "His name shall be called . . . *the Mighty God.*"

*The serenity of the name*

When the angel instructed Joseph concerning the naming of the Savior, he said, "Thou shalt call his name *Jesus:* for he shall save his people from their sins" (Matt. 1:21). The Mighty God was to be seen *in action.* What happened thereafter may be summarized under four headings. (1) *The Mighty God Overcoming Difficulties* (Mark 8:1-9). Innumerable problems confronted Jesus and His followers, but the Master was never nonplussed! The disciples were astounded when He miraculously fed the multitude. (2) *The Mighty God Overcoming Diseases* (Matt. 4:23-24). Jesus became known as the Great Physician, and no one ever questioned His right to the title. He was never confronted by a sickness He could not heal. There had been miracles in earlier ages, but no one ever healed *multitudes* in a moment. (3) *The Mighty God Overcoming Danger* (John 18:4-6). Continually throughout His life, enemies tried to kill the Lord, but His remarkable demonstration of power in the Garden of Gethsemane revealed He was omnipotent. (4) *The Mighty God Overcoming Death* (Luke 24:5-8). From the dawn of time, death had been the greatest enemy of mankind. Even the greatest careers terminated in a grave. Now, because of the finished work of Christ, believers can shout exultantly, "Because He lives, I shall live also."

# THE EVERLASTING FATHER

(ISAIAH 9:6)

This in all probability was the most difficult, the most inscrutable name ever given to the Savior. It was the name which, enshrouded in mystery, was never used! Countless sermons have been preached about the Fatherhood of God, and innumerable books have been written in which this theme was expounded. Nevertheless, *the fatherhood of Jesus* has seldom been mentioned. Yet, Isaiah predicted "His name shall be called . . . the everlasting Father." Evidently, the prophet wished to emphasize that the coming Messiah would not be a god among many others, but the *one and only God,* who from eternal ages had been the Father, or Benefactor, of everything that existed.

Arius, a Greek theologian, born in Libya, North Africa, came into prominence in the year A.D. 318 when he affirmed that, since Jesus was the *Son* of God, there was a time when He did not exist. He was only a created being to whom the Almighty delegated authority. This view was condemned by a council of bishops in the year A.D. 321 and again denounced by a larger council at Nicaea four years later. Thereafter, Arius was banished and his books were burned publicly. Unfortunately, his doctrines survived, and several modern sects continue to teach that Jesus was subservient to the one true God—Jehovah. They admit the Son was the best of the created beings, but he never was and never could be equal with the Supreme God.

*The startling description . . . "The everlasting Father" (Isa. 9:6)*

No man can be a father until he has produced a child. Since God, by creation, produced the human race, He was said to be the Father of everything that existed. The term "Father" was never applied to Jesus during His sojourn on earth. Job claimed to be "a father to the poor" (Job 29:16), and this probably meant he was their protector and helper. Fathers are expected to do at least three things for their families: *to plan, provide,* and *protect.* All these facets of truth were clearly seen in the relationship between God and the children of Israel. Jehovah planned that they should be His chosen people; throughout history He would provide for their needs and protect them when danger threatened their existence. Even though Jesus was never addressed as "Father", He, nevertheless, expressed all the characteristics of the relationship shared by God with the chosen people. What Jehovah had been to Israel, Christ was to His followers. A body had been prepared for Him, and with a separate identity He was able to set before the disciples a pattern they were expected to follow. Although He was equal in essence with the eternal God, *as a man* He set an example and taught men to pray, "Our Father, which art in heaven, Hallowed be thy name" (Luke 11:2). The doctrine of the Trinity had not then been revealed; Israel believed in *one God.*

*The Savior's deliberation (John 14:8-11)*

"Philip said unto [Jesus], Lord, shew us the Father, and it sufficeth us. Jesus saith unto him . . . he that hath seen me hath seen the Father. Believe me that I am in the Father, and the Father in me." It should be acknowledged that, unless the Lord meant what He said, He was mentally deranged. He claimed absolute affinity with God. They thought, spoke, and acted as *one person.* Had He meant anything less than was suggested, the Lord would have said so. Jesus had become their spiritual Father, Leader, and Benefactor. As God had planned, provided, and protected His people, so Jesus too would do all that and more for those who had been born into the new family. The disciples soon recognized that if they had special needs, there was hardly need to ask Jehovah; they asked Jesus and they never asked in vain.

*The saint's declaration (1 John 1:3)*

John said, "That which we have seen and heard declare we unto you, that ye also may have fellowship with us: and truly our fellowship is with the Father and with his Son, Jesus Christ." The apostle failed to see any difference between the two. When he thought of his heavenly Father, he saw Jesus. When he remembered his Savior, he rejoiced that God had been among men. The *Word,* who was God, had been made flesh. Basically, this was not a cause for amazement. God had come to earth when He came in the person of Melchizedek (Heb. 7:3) when He appeared to the parents of Samson (Judg. 13:22), and when He saved the Hebrew boys from the king's fire (Dan. 3:25). John had no difficulty in believing these facts. If he were ever amazed, it was when he wondered how he, a sinner, had been permitted to lean upon the bosom of God. That, after all, was a privilege only given by a Father to those who were precious in His sight.

# THE PRINCE OF PEACE

(ISAIAH 9:6)

"The Prince of Peace" is probably the most attractive of all the Lord's names. Peace, unfortunately, is one of the most elusive treasures known to man. The world is filled with discord, bitterness, enmity, and war. Instead of living together in harmony, nations invent and use weapons by which millions of innocent people perish. It has become the desire of every God-loving man and woman that somehow, someday, there will be a world in which suffering will be unknown. It is impossible to reach that goal without the assistance of the Prince of Peace. That is the most important lesson mankind needs to learn.

*The King of Peace . . . and righteousness (Heb. 7:2)*

When Abraham returned from his battle with the kings, he was met by a mysterious king, named Melchizedek, who was said to be the King of Salem (Heb. 7:2), and to this illustrious monarch Abraham gave tithes of all he possessed. Throughout the Scriptures the same name reappeared, and, finally, in the Epistle to the Hebrews, the author wrote strange and wonderful things. Melchizedek was "without father; without mother, without descent, having neither beginning of days [birth], nor end of life; but made like unto the Son of God; abideth a priest continually" (Heb. 7:3). Those who believe the Bible to be the Word of God consider this statement to be extremely important. It indicates Melchizedek was another of the theophanies mentioned in the Book of Genesis. Tithes were only given to God, and the fact that Melchizedek graciously accepted them from Abram suggests that he was more than an ordinary man. It is interesting to see that in the order of precedence, *righteousness* appears before *peace.* First and foremost, the mysterious One was righteous, and the natural consequence of this was tranquility and peace.

*The Prince of Peace . . . and redemption (Matt. 1:21)*

When we compare the scriptures, we cannot avoid the questions: "Did the King of Peace ever become the Prince of Peace? Were they basically the same person?" Isaiah, who predicted the coming of the Messiah, said, "For unto us *a child is born,* unto us *a son is given* . . . and his name shall be called . . . the Prince of Peace" (Isa. 9:6). As with Melchizedek *the Son* was "without father, without mother, without descent, having neither beginning of days, nor end of life. . . ." (Heb. 7:3). *The Child,* for whom a body was prepared, did have a beginning of days and died on a cross outside the walls of Jerusalem. The texts, therefore, become intriguing. It would be advantageous if we had more detailed answers to the questions concerning any relationship between (1) the ancient Melchizedek; (2) the One who was called "the Ancient of days" (Dan. 7:9), and (3) the Prince of Peace. God instructed Joseph that the Baby to be born should be called Jesus, "*for he shall save his people from their sins*" (Matt. 1:21). Peace would be established because redemption would be accomplished. The cross and the crown were inextricably woven together in the fabric of the divine will.

*The kingdom of peace . . . and reconciliation (Isa. 11:5-9)*

It would have been impossible to accompany Jesus on His journeys through Palestine without becoming aware of His serenity. He brought to men and women peace thought to be beyond their reach. He gave peace to those whose lives had been enslaved by evil and restored peace to multitudes whose guilt tormented their consciences. Jesus made enemies to become friends, but this did not exhaust His amazing ministry. Isaiah predicted that what the Prince of Peace did for individuals, He would eventually do for God's world. The prophet confidently predicted, "There shall come forth a rod out of the stem of Jesse . . . and the spirit of the Lord shall rest upon him. The wolf also shall dwell with the lamb, and the leopard shall lie down with the kid; and the calf and the young lion and the fatling together; and a little child shall lead them. They shall not hurt nor destroy in all my holy mountain: for the earth shall be full of the knowledge of the Lord, as the waters cover the sea. . . . *and his rest shall be glorious*" (Isa. 11:1-10). Only then, in the fullest sense, will Jesus be both the King and the Prince of Peace.

> Jesus shall reign where'er the sun,
> Doth his successive journeys run:
> His kingdom stretch from shore to shore,
> Till moons shall wax and wane no more.

# A ROOT OF JESSE . . . an ensign of the people

(ISAIAH 11:10)

Within Old Testament literature, the term "an ensign" had three different connotations. The uncertainty of its true meaning has always attracted students. It is a translation of three Hebrew words and thus conveys a variety of meanings. (1) It may have referred to a banner carried by a tribe into battle and thus could have represented a rallying point in times of adversity. (2) It could have been a sign of identification indicating the location of the tribe to which it belonged. (3) It could have been a banner, sign, flag, or signal on the top of a hill or pole. During the heat of a battle, sounds may not have been heard, but any banner flown from a tall pole would be easily seen, and a commander-in-chief would have been able to control the movement of his soldiers. There was also a custom of giving a banner to defeated foes. This was the guarantee of protection and represented an oath taken by the conqueror.

*The sign of recognition . . . an ensign of the people*

Each of the tribes of Israel had its own distinctive banner or ensign which was carried into battle. As long as it was held high, everyone knew its soldiers were still fighting. It expressed an even greater truth. The God of the tribe, Jehovah, was with His people in the struggle. This idea was amplified when the pillar of fire and the hovering cloud preceded Israel in the wilderness. The same truth was enunciated by the Captain of the Lord's hosts, who was the unseen but very present Helper, in all Israel's struggles (see Josh. 5:13-15). Without the assistance of God, Israel would have been completely vanquished. Yet, they were able to say, "If God be for us, who can be against us." The Lord was truly "an ensign for His people."

*The sign of rallying . . . "to it shall the Gentiles seek"*

This was an important statement made by Isaiah during an era of Hebrew conservatism. Gentiles were considered to be outcasts, "aliens from the commonwealth of Israel" (Eph. 2:12). In some senses, the root of Jesse seemed to be useless, unproductive, and dead. Yet, the prophet said that from the old root of Jesse would come a new growth; the root would produce new life to which even the unwanted Gentiles would be attracted. During conflicts when the enemy proved to be stronger than expected, weary soldiers, perhaps isolated from their comrades, looked to the ensign and, pressing closer, found friends struggling in the same cause. It was always better to be flanked by allies when confronting enemies. Together, Israel could stand and win; isolated, their chances of success diminished. The prophet's vision encompassed the world; he realized that God's love recognized no racial barriers. It was significant that after the defeat of the Amalekites, Moses built an altar and called it Jehovah-nissi. This meant, "The Lord is my banner" (Exod. 17:13-15).

*The sign of resting . . . "and his rest shall be glorious"*

Israel's foes were sometimes executed, but often when many were captured, they were given an ensign as a token of the goodwill of their conquerors. It became the sign of an oath which guaranteed protection. Isaiah envisaged the day when the Messiah would triumph over legions of Gentiles and when, captivated by the gospel of His grace, they would yield in submission at His feet. At first glance, the statement appears to present grammatical problems. Isaiah said, "To it shall the *Gentiles* seek, and *his* rest shall be glorious" (Isa. 11:10). Did he mean to imply that the Gentiles who yielded to Christ would discover that He provided a rest beyond their imagination? If that was the case, then the promise should be linked with another text found in Matthew 11:28. Jesus said, "Come unto me, all ye that labor and are heavy laden, *and I will give you rest.*" The Divine Conqueror guarantees protection for those who surrender to His will. Isaiah uttered amazing truths; he had a great source of information. God, who sees the end from the beginning, was pleased to reveal to His servant things which would ultimately come to pass.

# A RULER IN ZION; THE PRINCE OF KINGS

(JOHN 1:49; ISAIAH 24:23; REVELATION 1:5)

All the regal names of the Savior were interesting and thought-provoking, but Isaiah's statement was of special importance. He said: "The Lord of Hosts shall *reign in Mount Zion, and in Jerusalem*. . . " (Isa. 24:23). This text supplied a localized name; it referred to the city in which Jesus was crowned with thorns. When the angel announced the imminent birth of the Savior, he said to Mary: "And, behold, thou shalt conceive in thy womb, and bring forth a son, and shalt call his name Jesus. . . .and the Lord God shall give unto him *the throne of his father David*" (Luke 1:31-32). David reigned in Jerusalem, and if Jesus is to occupy *that* throne, He must return to earth. For many centuries the Jews have had no king (see Hos. 3:4). Yet, Zechariah, speaking of the closing days of time, said: "And the Lord shall be king over all the earth; in that day shall there be one Lord, and his name one" (Zech. 14:9).

*The Prince revealing*

John expressed a remarkable sequence of thought. As an introduction to the message to the seven churches in Asia, he sent greetings from "Jesus Christ. . .*the faithful witness,* and *the first-begotten of the dead,* and *the prince of the kings of the earth*" (Rev. 1:5). The apostle desired to express the past, present, and future ministries of the Lord. When Jesus preached in Palestine, He was the "Faithful Witness." After He had risen from the dead, He continued to minister in heaven. When He returns to reign upon the earth, the entire world will receive the greatest benediction ever bestowed by God. The eminent writer, Dr. Charles J. Rolls, in his book has a magnificent paragraph concerning the uniqueness of the Lord Jesus. "No Pharaoh of Egypt, no king of Babylon, no emperor of Persia, no philosopher of Greece, no Caesar of Rome, no sultan of Turkey, no caliph of Arabia, no czar of Russia, no kaiser of Germany, no Napoleon of France ever had a new lamp hung in the sky to mark his never-to-be-forgotten entry into this world" (*The World's Greatest Name*, p. 159).

*The Prince rising*

Throughout history, nations have known many monarchs. Some were great, like David and Solomon; others were failures like Saul and many of his descendants. Unfortunately, all of the kings died and remained dead. The writers of the New Testament were thrilled to announce that their King, the King of Israel, had died and risen again; He was the first to accomplish that astounding feat. Paul evidently had this thought in mind when he wrote to Timothy as follows: "Now unto the King eternal, *immortal,* invisible, the only wise God, be honor and glory forever and ever. Amen'' (1 Tim. 1:17).

*The Prince reigning*

God promised that His Son would reign in Jerusalem, and that to make this possible, Jesus must return to earth. John never forgot his Master's word and eventually supplied additional details concerning the millennial reign of Christ. He believed that the time would arrive when ''the earth shall be full of the knowledge of the Lord, as the waters cover the sea'' (Isa. 11:9). He envisaged the time when ''the wolf also shall dwell with the lamb, and the leopard shall lie down with the kid...and a little child shall lead them'' (Isaiah 11:6). When the kings of the nations kneel at His feet, Jesus will become *their* Prince.

*The Prince remaining*

''And he shall reign over the house of Jacob *forever;* and of his kingdom *there shall be no end''* (Luke 1:33). It is difficult to comprehend the vastness of eternity, but the Bible states that ''the Prince of Kings'' will establish an empire which will continue forever. Most of the earthly kingdoms have disappeared; only a few remain where a monarch occupies the throne of the nation. If the present trend continues, these could be in jeopardy. No enemy will ever overthrow the kingdom of Christ, for like its King it will be immortal. Happy will they be who share eternity with Him.

# THE CHIEF CORNERSTONE

(Isaiah 28:16; 1 Corinthians 10:4)

The size and strength of cornerstones used in ancient buildings continue to amaze modern engineers. How the ancient builders placed those large blocks in exalted positions remains an inscrutable mystery. It is still possible to see some of these stones, for archaeologists have uncovered these precious masterpieces. Some of the cornerpieces used in Solomon's temple were more than 38 feet long and exceeded a hundred tons in weight. It was not a cause for amazement when ancient buildings attracted the attention of the prophets. Isaiah, who saw Solomon's temple on many occasions, wrote: "Therefore, thus saith the Lord God, Behold I *lay* in Zion for a foundation a stone, a tried stone, a precious cornerstone, a sure foundation" (Isa. 28:16). Simon Peter, who lived centuries later, quoted that scripture and likened it to the Savior (1 Peter 2:6). Paul wrote of a similar theme, "That Rock was Christ" (1 Cor. 10:4).

*The stone that suggests*

God said through His servant Isaiah: "Behold I *lay* in Zion for a foundation a stone." He did not create it, He did not prepare it! He took that which already existed and placed it where it could perform its divinely appointed mission. Evidently, Isaiah used the imagery of stones cut from the mountains and prepared by men for their position in the temple of Solomon. God spoke of another structure, a *living* temple, in which men and women would be living stones. The foundation of that building would be the Rock of Ages! He would not *come into being;* that is, He would not be prepared by human hands. He who had been from eternity would be "laid" in a new position to accomplish something never before attempted.

*The stone that supports*

It was essential that huge stones be obtained for Israel's temple, for the weight to be supported was almost beyond estimation. Situated on the crest of a hill, the structure had to rest solidly on strong foundations; otherwise it would have slid into the valley. The temple erected by King Solomon was threatened by time and circumstances and, ultimately, was destroyed forever. The spiritual temple of which the New Testament preachers spoke was a building which cannot be destroyed. The stone which the builders rejected became the headstone of the corner, and as Peter said, ". . .he that believeth on him shall not be confounded" (1 Peter 2:6). Paul also referred to this dependable foundation when he wrote: "Other foundation can no man lay than that is laid, which is Jesus Christ" (1 Cor. 3:11).

*The stone that shelters*

Ira D. Sankey made famous a song which expressed this idea.

> The Lord's our Rock, in Him we hide;
> A shelter in the time of storm.
> Secure whatever ill betide,
> A shelter in the time of storm.
> Oh, Jesus is a Rock in a weary land:
> A shelter in the time of storm.

Most people have known the experience of sheltering behind a cornerstone. Probably that was one of the reasons why Peter wrote that Jesus was *precious.* A free translation of the passage might be, "He that dependeth on Him shall not be disappointed."

*The stone that strengthens*

Writing to the church at Ephesus, Paul declared, "Now therefore ye are no more strangers and foreigners, but fellowcitizens with the saints, and of the household of God; and are built upon the foundation of the apostles and prophets, *Jesus Christ himself being the chief cornerstone;* in whom all the building fitly framed together groweth unto a holy temple in the Lord: in whom ye also are builded together for an habitation of God through the Spirit" (Eph. 2:19-22). Unity is the secret of strength; cracks in a wall are the forerunners of disaster. Paul expressed the unity of the Church when he wrote: "Where there is neither Greek nor Jew, circumcision nor uncircumcision, Barbarian, Scythian, bond nor free: but Christ is all, and in all" (Col. 3:11). A cornerstone unites walls in which stones are cemented together to make a complete structure. The true Church is completely dependent upon the Lord who created it. Without the cornerstone, there would be no building; without the Chief Cornerstone, there would be no Church. Christians owe everything to their Savior.

> On Christ the solid Rock I stand,
> All other ground is sinking sand.

# THE WAY

(ISAIAH 35:8; JOHN 14:6)

If the Old Testament Scriptures were compared to a mountain range, the thirty-fifth chapter of Isaiah would be one of its most attractive peaks. There the prophet described the wonder of Israel's future and indicated how the blessing of God would come to His people. Isaiah's message thrilled the souls of all who believed Jesus to be the Messiah.

*The way. . .predicted*

"Then the eyes of the blind shall be opened, and the ears of the deaf shall be unstopped. Then shall the lame man leap as an hart, and the tongue of the dumb sing: for in the wilderness shall waters break out, and streams in the desert. And the parched ground shall become a pool, and the thirsty land springs of water: in the habitations of dragons, where each lay, shall be grass with reeds and rushes. *And an highway shall be there, and a way, and it shall be called The way of holiness*" (Isa. 35:5-8). This was one of the most delightful utterances made by any of the prophets. It was a light shining in the darkness, a beacon encouraging the weary to continue their pilgrimage. That text has been translated in several ways: "A clear way shall be there," "A well-marked way shall be there," "A trodden way shall be there." Evidently, the prophet desired to emphasize that it would be impossible not to recognize the highway; many travelers would be using it.

*The way. . .proclaimed*

When the Savior spoke of the many mansions to be found in heaven, He said to His listeners, "And whither I go ye know, and the way ye know. Thomas saith unto him, Lord, we know not whither thou goest; and how can we know the way? Jesus saith unto him, *I am the way,* the truth, and the life: no man cometh unto the Father, but by me" (John 14:4-6). Evidently, the Lord planned to provide more than Isaiah predicted. It was true that through the power of His ministry, the lame were made to walk, the dumb to speak, and even the dead were raised. Nevertheless, the Lord not only provided blessings for this life; He also promised eternal deliverance for those who followed Him. The Lord claimed to be the way by which people could obtain eternal happiness. He was the *known way,* the *clearly marked way,* the highway along which human traffic moved freely.

*The way. . .procured*

The term "the way" became one of the most used definitions of all who preached the gospel. They recognized their Lord to be the highway leading to many places. For example, the writer to the Hebrews emphasized the privileges of Christians. He wrote: "Having therefore, brethren, boldness to enter into the holiest by the blood of Jesus, *by a new and living way,* which he hath consecrated for us, through the veil, that is to say, his flesh" (Heb. 10:19-20). Throughout the ages, the high priest alone enjoyed the privilege of approaching the mercy seat. Ordinary people never knew that experience. Isaiah indicated that no man would be prevented from walking the new highway. Even fools, so he said, would not be forbidden access to the presence of God (see Isa. 35:8).

*The way. . .practiced*

The early believers in Christ were called Christians, but they were known first as "followers of the Way." When Saul of Tarsus sought permission to persecute the disciples of Jesus, he referred to them as being "of this way" (Acts 9:2). Prior to the riot in Ephesus, the enemies of Paul "spake evil of *that way* before the multitude" (Acts 19:9). When Paul gave his testimony before Felix it was said of the royal listener that he had *"more perfect knowledge of that way"* (Acts 24:22). It was recognized that Jesus of Nazareth had created something new; His doctrines were different from all others. His power was unique in that He and His followers healed the sick; His demands included loyalty and righteousness. Social status was basically unimportant; what people *were* was of more value than their possessions. They were voluntarily walking along a highway of truth which Jesus had created. They were followers of *the Way.* They were pilgrims and not hoboes! Their destination was assured, they knew where they were going! Blessed are the people who know the road so well; they have no need of signposts!

# THE BRINGER OF GOOD TIDINGS

(Isaiah 41:27)

Throughout the history of the Church, theologians have argued about the authenticity of the book of the prophet Isaiah. Many have claimed that there were *two* Isaiahs, for one author could not have written the entire manuscript. They have emphasized the fact that the first thirty-nine chapters described judgment, righteousness and law. The next twenty-seven chapters spoke of comfort, mercy, forgiveness, and grace. Apparently, they never considered the astonishing idea that the writings of Isaiah were a miniature Bible within the larger one. The first thirty-nine chapters represent the thirty-nine books of the Old Testament; the next twenty-seven represent the twenty-seven books of the New Testament. The second section began with the ministry of John the Baptist (see Isa. 40:1-3 and Matt. 3:3). It was and still is significant that the phrase "good news" is mentioned four times in this section of the prophet's writings (Isa. 40:9; 41:27; 52:7; 61:1). God's promise was a source of inspiration to all believers in Israel. He said, "I will give to Jerusalem *one that bringeth good tidings.*"

*The authoritative message (Isa. 40:8-11)*

The prophet wrote: "The grass withereth, the flower fadeth: but the word of our God shall stand forever. O Zion, that bringest good tidings, get thee up into the high mountain; O Jerusalem, that bringest good tidings, lift up thy voice with strength; lift it up, be not afraid; say unto the cities of Judah, Behold your God! Behold, *the Lord God will come*....He shall feed his flock like a shepherd...." Amid the decadence and despair in Israel, these promises shone as stars in a dark sky. Material things would perish, but the promises of God would last eternally. Israel, therefore, could be assured that God — *The Bringer of good tidings* — would come to His people. His forgiving grace would banish their sins; His unlimited power, deliver them from their enemies; His abundant provision, safeguard their future. The cities of Judah were not to despair. They were commanded to lift up their voices to proclaim the good news of their gospel.

*The angelic message (Luke 2:9-10)*

The night was a little chilly; the sheep were quietly resting; the shepherds were gathered around their fire. Far away in the heavens the stars twinkled, and everything seemed to be peaceful in God's world. And then, suddenly, a strange but wonderful sound reached the ears of the startled listeners. "And lo, the angel of the Lord came upon them, and the glory of the Lord shone round about them; and they were sore afraid. And the angel said unto them, Fear not;

for, behold, I bring you good tidings of great joy, which shall be to all people, for unto you is born this day in the city of David a Savior, which is Christ the Lord." *God* had come to His people! That in itself was sufficient reason for men to rejoice. Isaiah addressed his remarks to the inhabitants of Judah, but the angels spoke of "good tidings of great joy, which shall be *to all people"* irrespective of their nationality or color.

*The amazing message (Isa. 61:1; Luke 4:17-20)*

The people in the synagogue at Nazareth were very attentive. Jesus, the carpenter, whom they had known for many years, was about to read the Scripture. They watched as He took the scroll and listened as He read: "The Spirit of the Lord is upon me, because he has anointed me to preach the gospel [*euaggelizesthai*—to announce glad tidings, good news] to the poor; he hath sent me to heal the brokenhearted, to preach deliverance to the captives, and recovering of sight to the blind, to set at liberty them that are bruised, to preach the acceptable year of the Lord. *And he closed the book. . . ."* It was significant that Jesus ceased reading at that point. Had He read the next statement from Isaiah's prophecy, He would have said: "and the day of vengeance of our God." Christ had come with "good tidings"; *the day of judgment had not arrived!* His wonderful ministry brought hope to the hopeless, healing to the sick, sight to the blind, the ability to walk to those who were lame, and, best of all, salvation to undeserving sinners. People loved to listen to His message for He was truly a *bringer of good tidings*.

# GOD'S SERVANT

(ISAIAH 42:1-2; PHILIPPIANS 2:6-7)

The name "God's Servant", which was given by God the Father to His Son, may not appear to be as glamorous as many of the Lord's other titles, but when its implications are considered, it is probably among the most dignified and choice appellations of the Savior. Since the beginning of time, God has had many servants who delighted to obey His commands. Angels and prophets were among those honored with a divine commission. The sacred records tell of their faithful endeavors. Occasionally, some men failed in their assignments, and their actions led to disastrous conclusions. Jesus was different; no other belonged to His category. God said, "Behold my servant; whom I uphold; mine elect, in whom my soul delighteth. I have put my Spirit upon him; he shall bring forth judgment to the Gentiles. He shall not cry, nor lift up, nor cause his voice to be heard in the street." *(He shall not be a rabble-rouser!)* Here may be found all the characteristics of true ordination.

*Divinely chosen . . . "Behold my servant. . . mine elect"*

God's servants are never alone; He remains their abiding Companion. The Lord speaking to Ezekiel said, "And I sought for a man among them, that should make up [repair] the hedge, and stand in the gap before me for the land, that I should not destroy it: *but I found none"* (Ezek. 22:30). Abraham interceded with Jehovah regarding the sparing of Sodom and Gomorrah; unfortunately, he failed "to stand in the gap," with the result that the cities of the plains perished (see Gen. 18:23-33). It is thrilling to know that when all others failed, Christ stepped down from His throne of splendor to "stand in the gap" for a lost world. Like Abraham, He could not find worthiness in the sons of men; as a result, adopting new methods, He took their sins to the cross and made forgiveness possible. The pride of Jehovah echoed in His statement: "Behold my servant. . . *in whom my soul delighteth."* Jesus was the only One worthy in heaven and earth, and God chose Him to do what, for others, was completely impossible. Nothing has changed; He was the only one worthy at the beginning of history; He will be the only one worthy at its end (see Rev. 5:5-9).

*Daily controlled . . . "I have put my Spirit upon him"*

A faithful servant lives to carry out the wishes of his master. Personal ambition never supersedes the urge to justify the confidence exhibited by his employer. This characteristic was constantly in evidence throughout the ministry of the Savior. He was baptized of the Spirit, was led into the wilderness by the same Spirit, and afterward in the synagogue at Nazareth said, "The Spirit of the

Lord is upon me..." (Luke 4:1,14,18). Joshua described how "The captain of the LORD's host" came to be the unseen commander of Israel's army (5:14). Unfortunately, the children of Israel did not pay attention to what the Lord commanded, and their negligence caused continuing problems. On the contrary, the Lord Jesus was completely surrendered to the guidance of God and daily followed the suggestions made by the Holy Spirit. He set an example which all Christians should emulate.

*Delightfully concerned... "A bruised reed shall he not break"*

"A bruised reed shall he not break, and the smoking flax shall he not quench" (Isa. 42:3). This became one of the greatest illustrations supplied by the prophet. A reed was a type of pen used by writers, but occasionally the tip of the reed became soft and unreliable. A little pressure produced a smudge or blot on the parchment. Such pens were discarded. The flax was the equivalent of a wick in a candle. Sometimes it needed to be trimmed so badly that the flame would almost die. Impatient men might be tempted to snuff it out! God's true Servant would be gentle and careful. When men, like reeds, were unreliable, His love would nurse them back to health—repair them! If the flame of devotion within the human breast were in danger, He would gently restore its vitality. All this was included in the commission given to God's trusted Servant. "I the LORD have called thee in righteousness...to open the blind eyes, to bring out the prisoners from the prison, and them that sit in darkness out of the prison house" (Isa. 42:6-7). Evidently God planned to redeem sinners. The task of liberation was entrusted to God's anointed Servant. It was and still is significant that God said of His Servant, "*He* shall not fail" (see Isa. 42:4).

# A MAN OF SORROWS

(Isaiah 53:3)

It has often been claimed that an artist is best known through his works. The soul of a painter is seen in his paintings; the heart of a singer is heard through his songs. Similarly, it might be said that the creation is a mirror in which may be seen the reflection of God. Dr. Frank Boreham once asked, "Can anyone imagine the Creator of a kitten being unable to laugh?" Is it possible to hear the enchanting song of a lark and not hear the echoes of eternal melodies? If God made the birds to sing, the flowers to bloom, and the sunset to be resplendent with glorious beauty, surely He must appreciate things which are lovely. Job realized this when God asked: "Where wast thou when I laid the foundations of the earth?... When the morning stars sang together, and all the sons of God shouted for joy?" (Job 38:4-7). At that time it would have been impossible to believe that the face of the Creator would become disfigured by agony.

*Disappointed by His people*

There are occasions when a wound in one's soul is more painful than a blow to the body. A mother may never weep or complain but her eyes may reveal an intense sorrow destroying her life. The moral collapse of a son or daughter may cause more anguish than any physical attack. John wrote, "He came unto his own, and his own received him not" (John 1:11). The Savior spoke of a husbandman who sent his servants to gather the fruits of his vineyard, but when they were assaulted by the workmen, "he sent unto them his son, saying, They will reverence my son. But when the husbandmen saw the son, they said among themselves, This is the heir; come, let us kill him" (see Matt. 21:33-41). Probably, it will never be known how intense was the Lord's sorrow and disappointment when He was rejected by His people.

*Disfigured by His pain*

Isaiah wrote, "His visage was so marred more than any man..." (Isa. 52:14). The literal rendering of the text suggests that the Lord's face was marred beyond recognition. When Jesus was beaten by the Roman soldiers, flesh was torn from His body, and He endured torture of the worst kind. Many criminals never survived the scourging; they died at the whipping post. So intense was the strain imposed upon the Lord that even in the Garden of Gethsemane blood and perspiration mingled on His brow. The terrible pain reached its climax when nails were driven through His hands and feet and the cross dropped into a prepared hole in the ground. The crime of the crucifixion was unjustified, and the world now condemns what was done long ago.

*Distressed by His problem*

"Yet it pleased the Lord to bruise him. . ." (Isa. 53:10). Humans are incapable of understanding all that Jesus suffered. He bore a heavier burden and fought a greater fight than can be appreciated. The Son of God voluntarily accepted our sin and carried it to the tree. The darkness which covered the land was indicative of the shadow which fell when an eternal fellowship was broken. The prophet Habakkuk wrote: "Thou art of purer eyes than to behold evil, and canst not look on iniquity" (Hab. 1:13). When the Lord took our sins to His cross, God turned away His face, and that awful experience is beyond comprehension. It is significant that when the darkness ended Jesus cried, "My God, my God, why hast thou forsaken me?" Matthew used the aorist tense of the Greek verb and actually wrote: "Why *didst* thou forsake me?" That tense denotes something *completed in the past.* The work had been *finished*; the Lord's cry was one of unspeakable relief. Yet, we shall never be able to understand how intense was the darkness through which Christ passed.

*Delighted with His purpose*

It has been claimed by heretics that Jesus was the unfortunate victim of a Jewish mob and that He died in despair and shame upon a criminal's cross. That conclusion appears to be strange when compared with Hebrews 12:2, "Looking unto Jesus. . . who for the joy that was set before him endured the cross, despising the shame, and is set down at the right hand of the throne of God." The resurrection was the light at the end of the tunnel. Although Jesus became the Man of Sorrows, He never lost sight of the fact that His sufferings were temporal; His joy would be eternal. He embraced our darkness that we who already live in the shadow of death might enter into a realm where darkness, sorrow, and death are unknown.

Man of Sorrows! What a name<br>
For the Son of God who came;<br>
Ruined sinners to reclaim.<br>
Hallelujah! What a Savior.

# THE MESSIAH

(DANIEL 9:25; JOHN 1:41; JOHN 4:25)

*Messiah* was the greatest word in the Hebrew vocabulary. It expressed the most vital element of Jewish theology and excited the people's hope of the miraculous deliverance expected from the anointed messenger of God. Throughout centuries of oppression and servitude, the nation expectantly looked forward to the time when God's chosen servant would break the shackles of bondage and lift Israel to heights of grandeur and dominion which would be the envy of all nations.

*The Prince. . . coming*

Among the most important of the ancient prophets was Daniel, who wrote: "Know therefore and understand, that from the going forth of the commandment to restore and to build Jerusalem unto the Messiah the Prince shall be seven weeks, and threescore and two weeks. . . .And after threescore and two weeks shall Messiah be cut off, but not for himself" (Dan. 9:25-26). Sir Robert Anderson in his monumental book *The Coming Prince* (Kregel Publications), proved that the stipulated time was fulfilled the day Christ rode into Jerusalem. Soon after that memorable occasion, the Lord Jesus was indeed "cut off," but not for himself. A prince is an uncrowned son of a royal family. The Jewish people might have crowned Jesus with gold; instead, they used thorns as a substitute! Nevertheless, Daniel expressed the hope of his nation. Rabbis encouraged listeners to anticipate that glorious event, and teachers reminded their students that the messianic promise was the chief hope of the oppressed nation. Unfortunately, the people had cataracts in their eyes, their vision was blurred, they failed to recognize Him; and He died upon a cross which they supplied.

*The Preacher. . . calling*

Describing one of the earliest events in the ministry of the Lord, John wrote: "Andrew first findeth his own brother Simon, and saith unto him, We have found the Messiah. . . .And he brought him to Jesus." Later, when another man came before the Lord, he (Nathaniel) said, "Rabbi, thou art the Son of God; thou art the King of Israel. . . " (John 1:41-42 and 49). Evidently, at that time Jesus was not the King of Israel, but no doubt existed in the consciousness of Nathaniel. He was certain of his faith, and for him, at least, Jesus had already been crowned in the heart of His new convert. Evidently, faith filled the heart of Nathaniel; he was seeing that which had not come to pass. Blessed is the person who sees, in a few moments, what others fail to recognize in a lifetime.

*The Prophet . . . claiming*

Embarrassed by a revelation of former indiscretion, the Samaritan woman said, "Sir, I perceive that thou art a prophet," and wishing to change the subject of the conversation, mentioned religion. She said, "I know that Messiah cometh, which is called Christ; when he is come, he will tell us all things. Jesus saith unto her, *I that speak unto thee, am he*" (John 4:19 and 25). This was one of the many claims made by the Savior, and there was no ambiguity in the statement. Honest students must admit Christ either was or was not what He claimed. He asserted that He was the fulfillment of the Messianic predictions. He was the King of Israel.

Writing to Timothy and referring to the Savior, Paul wrote: "Now unto the King eternal, immortal, invisible, the only wise God, be honor and glory, forever and ever" (1 Tim. 1:17). When Saul of Tarsus, one of the most antagonistic Jews of his generation, recognized Jesus to be the long-awaited Messiah, his entire life was transformed: and, becoming the apostle to the Gentiles, he published his message throughout the known world. It is impossible to love and serve Christ and not be enthusiastic about bringing others to Him. People who have no interest in the extension of the kingdom cannot be devoted to the King.

# THE BRANCH

(ZECHARIAH 6:12)

Branches were very common in Israel. The land was filled with vineyards, and forests covered the hillsides. With the possible exception of the men who supervised the growth of these valuable assets, few people exhibited interest in branches, until the prophets began uttering strange predictions. All the Hebrews believed that the Messiah would come to deliver Israel, but they never expected Him to have such a common name as "The Branch." The people understood illustrious names such as the King of Israel, the Prince of Peace, and the Star out of Jacob, but to liken their Deliverer to a branch appeared ridiculous. Isaiah said, "In that day shall the branch of the LORD be beautiful and glorious" (4:2). He also said the Branch would grow out of the root of Jesse (11:1). Jeremiah, on two occasions, called the coming Messiah "a righteous Branch" (23:5 and 33:15). Zechariah gave new dimensions to the name when he said the Branch would be the Servant of the living God (3:8), and would build the temple of the Lord (6:12). This common, yet glorious name, therefore deserves special consideration.

*The identity of the Branch*

God said, "Behold, I will bring forth *my servant, the branch.*" Branches are special in that they have a separate identity. The branches of a vine are not produced by an oak tree, and those of a thorn bush do not grow out of a cedar tree. Each plant or tree produces its own type of branch through which to express itself. It was to be expected that since the Messiah would be God's *branch,* the same type of life existing in the Almighty would flow through the divine representative. It would be impossible to differentiate between the life of the tree and the branch. They would be identical in essence. Either would express the other. The prophets knew that God could manifest Himself in numerous ways, but in the greatest matter of importance, He would only have one servant, who would be the Branch.

*The instrumentality of the Branch*

"THE BRANCH. . .shall build the temple of the Lord" (Zech. 6:12). It must be recognized that without branches a tree is helpless. This was the predominant truth taught when God gave to the Messiah the new name. Jehovah could never be completely helpless unless He chose to be! It may be said He placed Himself in that position when He appointed the Son to be His Representative. Jesus said, "For the Father judgeth no man, but hath committed all judgment unto the Son" (John 5:22). The Branch—Jesus—was the channel through whom God communicated His word, and expressed His wisdom. Whatever He desired to accomplish would be achieved through the Messiah, who would build the temple of the Lord. Christ would be God in action; Jesus would be the One to accomplish what had been planned before time began (see Rev. 13:8).

*The indispensability of the branch*

When Isaiah spoke of the blessedness of Israel's future, he said, "In that day shall the branch of the LORD be beautiful and glorious" (4:2) and "There shall come forth a rod out of the stem of Jesse, and a Branch shall grow out of his roots" (11:1). When, from what appeared to be a dead root, a new growth appeared, it seemed a miracle had been performed. Since the roots of Israel had been nonproductive, the nation became idolatrous and was carried captive into Babylon, so that any thought of future blessedness seemed unjustified. The prophet was aware of these disappointing features but knew the faithfulness of God never changed. The Almighty would move upon the apparently dead roots of Jesse, and from the ancient tribe would arise a Deliverer beyond compare. He would be beautiful and glorious! No one would supersede Him; no person would ever take His place. The Messiah would be completely indispensable in everything attempted by the living God. Thus did the prophet announce the scintillating attractiveness of the appointed Messiah. Yet, it remained inconceivable that, in spite of the clarity of the inspired message, Israel remained indifferent to the claims of Christ. Their crime never changed the fact that "The Branch of righteousness" (Jer. 33:15) remained the appointed channel through whom the grace of God reached the souls of sinful men.

My hope is built on nothing less
Than Jesus' blood and righteousness.
I dare not trust the sweetest frame,
But wholly lean on Jesus' name.
All other ground is sinking sand.

# THE MESSENGER OF THE COVENANT

(MALACHI 3:1)

Malachi, the last of the Old Testament prophets, definitely referred to John the Baptist and Jesus when he wrote, "Behold, I will send my messenger, and he shall prepare the way before me: and the Lord, whom ye seek, shall suddenly come to his temple, even the messenger of the covenant, whom ye delight in." That prediction was fulfilled when John the Baptist was followed by Jesus, who cleansed *His* temple (John 2:13-17). The prophet described the Coming One as "The messenger of the covenant," a definition which invites investigation. W. E. Vine states that the word *diatheegee* signifies "a disposition of property by will or otherwise." God covenanted to do certain things for the children of Israel. His "document" bore the divine signature; the Messenger of the covenant would arrive to transact business relative to that arrangement.

*The covenant recorded (Deut. 29:1)*

When Moses brought to Israel the commandments of the Almighty, the people listened to the words of their leader and entered into a covenant of mutual understanding. God promised to accompany His people in their journeys, meet their needs, and solve their problems. The nation promised to serve the only true God, observe His statutes, and teach their children to follow their example. Throughout the centuries which followed, God honored His side of the agreement, but Israel did not. They worshiped idols and permitted unlawful practices to thrive within the nation. Yet, time after time God forgave their sins, pardoned their indiscretions, and delivered them from oppressors. Israel repented but, alas, soon returned to their waywardness.

*The covenant reminder (Mal. 3:1-2)*

"Behold I will send my messenger, . . . But who may abide the day of his coming? and who shall stand when he appeareth? For he is like a refiner's fire, and like fuller's soap. . . . For I am the LORD, I change not; *therefore ye sons of Jacob are not consumed*" (Mal. 3:1-2, 6). Malachi contrasts the unchanging faithfulness of God with the inconsistency of Israel. He stated that the *Messenger of the covenant* would arrive in His temple to remove its filth. The nation was supposed to delight in the covenant; they professed pride in being God's chosen people; and yet, their sinful practices dishonored the Lord and defiled His house. Malachi's prediction was fulfilled when Jesus arrived in the temple. He drove out the moneychangers, overthrew their tables and said, "Take these things hence; make not my Father's house an house of merchandise"

(John 2:16). The Lord constantly reminded His hearers that Israel, by every legal argument, had forfeited the right to be called the chosen people. This fact introduced a startling change. The old covenant was to be replaced by a new one.

*The covenant replaced (Heb. 9:14-15)*

"And for this cause he is the mediator of *the New Testament* [Covenant]. . . ." The writer also referred to *The Second Covenant.* "For if that first covenant had been faultless, then should no place have been sought for the second" (Heb. 8:7). Finally, the writer called the new covenant a *better* one. "Jesus made a surety of a better covenant" (Heb. 7:22). Pride made it difficult for the Jewish people to accept this information; they were reluctant to admit that they had not observed their part of the contract made with Jehovah. Yet, unbiased thinking agreed that the new covenant was infinitely superior to the old one. Formerly only Jews were permitted to participate in the service of the Almighty; now all nations would be welcomed into the embrace of Jehovah. The *God of Israel* was about to become *the Heavenly Father* of all who believed in His saving grace. This was the good news announced by God's messenger of the new covenant. Believers would become residences for the Holy Spirit, and deep within their affections, Christ would be crowned King.

# A REFINER AND PURIFIER OF SILVER

(MALACHI 3:3)

The art of refining is the process of removing impurities from metals, but within the Bible the term is also used to describe other occupations. The basic meaning of the ancient verb was *to distil* or *to strain.* Job mentioned the distilling of water (Job 36:27-28), and Isaiah spoke of the refining of wine (Isa. 25:6). The altar of incense was made of refined gold (1 Chron. 28:18) and when the Lord, through John, addressed the church in Laodicea, He urged them to purchase and appreciate *refined gold* (Rev. 3:18). Evidently, the value or art of refining in all spheres was the removal of impurities. When Malachi described the Messiah as a Refiner and Purifier, he introduced to Israel a conception as new as it was provocative. Most of the other prophets wrote of Christ's coming to *conquer;* Malachi stressed His coming to *cleanse!*

*His unique plan*

The ancient art of refining necessitated certain things. First, the ore had to be melted to liquid form, and then impurities were extracted. It has been claimed the ultimate test of perfection was the refiner's ability to see his image in the liquid metal. A true refiner would never be satisfied with anything less. Evidently God was more concerned with the righteousness of His people than with their deliverance from the thraldom of enemies. Israel looked for a Messiah who would deliver them from slavery; God looked for a clean, wholesome nation worthy of deliverance. Isaiah was aware of God's methods. He wrote: "Behold, I have refined thee, but not with silver; *I have chosen thee in the furnace of affliction*" (Isa. 48:10). Sometimes God's fires were *exceedingly hot!* To remove the impurity of idolatry from Israel, He permitted them to be almost consumed in the fires of Babylon. It was during their time of captivity that Israel learned to detest idols.

*His unwavering patience*

It was never easy for God to watch the suffering of His disappointing people. Yet, as a Refiner, He necessarily had to await the arrival of the exact moment when action became imperative. The removal of impurities from the molten metal could not be successfully accomplished until the ore was heated to the correct degree. A master refiner knew how long he had to wait, and his patience was produced by wisdom. When God delivered Isaac from the altar of sacrifice (Gen. 22:11-13), He appeared to be very late in going to the rescue of the lad, but *He was not too late!* God knows what He is doing!

*His unequaled perception*

The refiner waits to see the reflection of his image in the molten metal so that he can tell that the process of purification is nearing completion. Probably the poet understood this when he wrote,

> Lord Jesus Christ, grow Thou in me;
> And all things else recede.
> My heart be daily nearer Thee,
> From sin be daily freed.

Doubtless, this scripture was at least partially fulfilled when the Savior drove the traders out of the temple (John 2:13-17). Jeremiah referred to the bellows used in the heating of the ore (Jer. 6:29). Electricity was unknown in ancient days; therefore, blacksmiths and refiners supervised every detail connected with their fire. It would be of incomparable worth if men realized that God still controls the "bellows." No puff or wind or increase of fire can touch them without His permission. The hand that controls the apparatus is called *love.*

*His unsurpassed pleasure*

The pleasure of the refiner would be unmistakable as he beheld his finished product. John predicted that the saints would see Christ's face (Rev. 22:4), while poets throughout all ages have composed sonnets of praise to honor that moment. Yet, by the same token, may we not assume that the Lord will experience even greater happiness when He beholds those whom He has perfected? Paul wrote in Ephesians 4:12 of "the perfecting of the saints" and later in the same epistle (5:27) described how Christ will present to Himself the Church "not having spot or wrinkle, or any such thing; but that it should be holy and without blemish." It will only be then that once again the Lord will be able to say, "It is finished!"

# THE SUN OF RIGHTEOUSNESS

(Malachi 4:2)

The children of Israel endured many gloomy periods when despair permeated their thoughts, enslaved their spirits, and turned the future into a bleak and desolate wilderness. The land was always threatened by invasion, but the long captivity in Babylon ruined their aspirations. Their ancestors had been slaves in Egypt, a harrowing servitude that left scars on the soul of the nation. Israel's anguish did not decrease when prophets predicted the approach of darker periods of oppression. Roman invaders would subjugate the nation, while in the end of time, two-thirds of the people would perish. It was against that somber background that Malachi made his thrilling prediction. He said that after years of national distress, the Sun of righteousness would arise with healing in His wings. The hopeless would find hope, suffering people would be healed, and the defenseless would discover a haven of safety.

*The choice company . . . "you that fear my name"*

In spite of national oppression, Jehovah always had people who looked for the dawn. When Elijah believed that he alone represented God, he was told that there were seven thousand souls who had not bowed before Baal (see 1 Kings 19:18). People who feel neglected and alone should look around. There are others who share the faith and whose courage and loyalty might be a source of continuing delight. Malachi wrote: "Then they that feared the Lord spake often one to another; and the Lord hearkened, and heard it, and a book of remembrance was written before him for them that feared the Lord, and that thought upon his name. And they shall be mine, saith the Lord of Hosts, in that day when I make up my jewels; and I will spare them, as a man spareth his own son that serveth him" (Mal. 3:16-17). God is not unmindful of the trials of His people. He knows that continuing difficulties threaten the peacefulness of the soul. Yet, He knows what the end will be, and blessed are they who share His knowledge.

*The coming Christ . . . "the Sun of righteousness shall arise"*

This was true when Israel was beginning to ask: "Will Messiah ever come?" The Babe of Bethlehem was the answer to their question. It will be true when, after the unprecedented trials of the tribulation, the Lord Jesus returns to be the King of His people. Isaiah, describing the glory of that day, declared, "And righteousness shall be the girdle of his loins, and faithfulness the girdle of his reins. The wolf also shall dwell with the lamb, and the leopard shall lie down with the kid, and the calf and the young lion and the fatling together; and a little child shall lead them. . . . They shall not hurt nor destroy in all my holy mountain: for the earth shall be full of the knowledge of the Lord, as the waters cover the sea" (Isa. 11:5-6, 9).

It will be easy for the Sun of Righteousness to arise with healing in His wings; He has had a lot of practice throughout the ages!

*The continuing calm . . . "with healing in his wings"*

Perhaps Malachi was inspired by the fact that within the ancient tabernacle, the cherubims spread their wings over the mercy seat. Beneath, and in the center of those wings, God dwelt. Before that hallowed throne the high priest of Israel interceded for his people. It was a place of peace! The rising Sun with outstretched wings indicated that beneath those wings a trusting suppliant could find all his soul required. Possibly the writers of the Gospels remembered these facts when they saw Jesus touch a leper. It would have been impossible for a leper to see a greater sunrise than he saw in the face of the Savior. The Lord Jesus said, "I am the light of the world: he that followeth me shall not walk in darkness, but shall have the light of life" (John 8:12). Even the blind beggar testified, "One thing I know, that, whereas I was blind, now I see" (John 9:25). People who watch a sunrise have no wish to return to darkness.

# THE SON OF DAVID

(MATTHEW 1:17; 15:22; LUKE 18:38)

All Jews believed that the Messiah would come from the genealogical line of David. Therefore, Matthew, who believed his Master to be the Messiah, deliberately traced the lineage of his Lord, so that critical opponents of Jesus would have no legal base for their accusations. It became increasingly noticeable that ordinary people used the royal title and made it the focal point in their appeals for assistance. They knew that David had been the King of Israel whose authority and power were unassailable. His Son, Jesus of Nazareth, was also the ruler of Israel, whose power overcame disease, banished blindness, and outlawed impossibilities. He was a legal descendant of David and was eligible to claim the throne of his forefather. God also recognized this fact when He said to Mary: "And, behold, thou shalt conceive in thy womb, and bring forth a son. . . .and the Lord God shall give unto him the throne of his father David: And he shall reign over the house of Jacob forever; and of his kingdom there shall be no end" (Luke 1:31-33).

*"Son of David". . .the cry of deception (Matt. 15:22)*

"And, behold, a woman of Canaan came out of the same coasts, and cried unto him, saying, Have mercy on me, O Lord, thou Son of David; my daughter is grievously vexed with a devil." It is significant that Matthew emphasized that the Gentile woman used words ordinarily spoken by a Jew or Jewess. David would not have been interested in *a woman of Canaan.* Evidently, fearing that Christ would not pay attention to her request, she deliberately decided to deceive the Lord by acting as though she were a Jewess. Jesus apparently ignored her request, and when the disciples reminded Him of her presence, His statement was remarkable. He seemed to insinuate that she was *a dog*—an outcast. Nevertheless, her cry indicated that although she was a Gentile, she believed in the royal ancestry of the Healer from Nazareth.

*"Son of David". . .the cry of desperation (Luke 18:38-39)*

The blind man was trembling; he had been informed that Jesus was near. He was unable to see, but the excitement of the crowd electrified his soul. Jesus could give sight to the blind and solve the problems of the beggar. Suddenly, he shouted, "Jesus, thou Son of David, have mercy on me." The Greek word used indicated this was a shouted request; an appeal for help. When the crowd urged him to remain silent, the man lost very valuable time. Believing his priceless opportunity might have passed, he was filled with desperation and he shouted again. To describe that incident, Luke used the word *ekrazen* which literally meant "the croak of a frog or raven."

His cry was inarticulate—a screech, a scream. The beggar discovered that Jesus was able to appreciate human need, however it was expressed. Once again it is noteworthy that even an impoverished beggar expressed the same faith. He believed that Jesus was the Son of David—the young king who never turned away helpless suppliants (see 1 Sam. 22:1-2).

*"Son of David". . .the cry of distinction (Luke 20:41-42; Ps. 110:1)*

The scribes were very silent since Jesus had outwitted them. Some did not believe in the resurrection of the dead, but Jesus had refuted their arguments, thus leaving them speechless. "And he said unto them, How say they that Christ is David's son? And David himself saith in the book of Psalms, The LORD said unto my Lord, Sit thou on my right hand, till I make thine enemies thy footstool. David therefore calleth him Lord, how is he then his son?" (Luke 20:41-44). When the scribes and Pharisees used the customary terminology, they expressed traditions; the common people using identical words expressed faith. Jesus was infinitely more than a descendant of David. The king of Israel was aware of the greatness of his successor and uttered words destined to become immortal. He referred to the Messiah as "my Lord." The expected Deliverer had been appointed to a place of eternal eminence, and if Jesus were indeed the Messiah, David would have been the first to fall at His feet. The scribes and Pharisees were blind and inexcusably bigoted; they deserved condemnation. As the Son of David Jesus was entitled to the throne of Israel; as the Son of God He could claim the throne of heaven; as Savior and Lord He is worthy to reign in the life of every redeemed soul.

# JESUS

(MATTHEW 1:21)

"And she shall bring forth a son, and shall call his name Jesus: for he shall save his people from their sins." Probably this was and continues to be the simplest and yet most sublime name known among men. It is occasionally given to persons in this age, but the glory and grace it represents are qualities which belong exclusively to Jesus of Nazareth. Before that wonderful name, kings and queens have bowed, innumerable books have been written which try to express the excellence of the One who bore it, and all over the world dedicated people live and die to proclaim it. It is the name which is above every name, and it is increasingly thought-provoking to remember that of the names available to God, He chose this one for His Son.

*The significance of the name*

*Jesus* is the New Testament equivalent of the Hebrew name "Joshua," the warrior who led Israel into Canaan. The ancient name meant "Jehovah is salvation." Probably, this fact made the name popular in Israel, so that throughout following centuries parents found pleasure in calling their sons Joshua. *Hosea* comes from the same root, and *Jehoshua* is yet another form of the same word. Haggai 1:14 states that it was given to the son of the high priest. Acts 7:45 and Hebrews 4:8 explain that the names of Joshua and Jesus were synonymous. It was to be expected, therefore, that some of the characteristics of the ancient leader would be reproduced in the life of the Savior. Joshua was never the king of Israel, but he was the undisputed leader of the tribes and in every sense was equal to a monarch. He was a prophet who spoke of the future and a priest who interceded for his people. It may or may not be significant that the three-fold characteristic of *prophet, priest,* and *king* was evident throughout the life of Israel's illustrious leader. When the Babe of Bethlehem was called Jesus (God is salvation), it became evident that He would be the fulfillment of these veiled predictions.

*The suggestiveness of the name*

"Thou shalt call his name Jesus: *for he shall save his people from their sins*" (Matt. 1:21). When Joshua saved his people from the thralldom of their enemies, his attention was directed toward militant aggressors who threatened the nation. Jesus was totally different in that He never attacked the Roman occupants of Palestine nor encouraged retaliation when attacks were made upon His followers. He advised that it would be better to forgive enemies rather than fight against them. The adversary lay within the souls of sinners.

Man's greatest enemy was himself; he needed to be delivered from the tyranny of evil. This was beyond the capability of Joshua or any other man. Jesus did something which was impossible for any other would-be deliverer. It became evident to all His followers that this was only accomplished through His death and resurrection. "Who his own self bare our sins in his own body on the tree, that we, being dead to sins, should live unto righteousness; by whose stripes ye were healed" (1 Peter 2:24). Jesus delivers from the *penalty, power,* and *presence* of sin. He is the complete Savior of those who trust in Him.

*The splendor of the name*

John Newton, who was lifted from depths of shame, wrote the immortal words:

> How sweet the Name of Jesus sounds,
> In a believer's ear:
> It soothes his sorrows, heals his wounds
> And drives away his fear.

The name of Jesus has charmed and thrilled people in all walks of life in every nation of the world. The greatest paintings made by the masters of their art depicted Christ. The greatest musicians ever known found inspiration as they tried to express their thoughts about Jesus. Handel's *Messiah* remains one of the greatest compositions ever made. The universities of all nations have libraries with innumerable books describing the Man who never attended an institute of learning. If everything that has been written, composed, or painted about Jesus of Nazareth were removed, the world would become impoverished. The name Jesus electrifies the imagination, stirs the soul, and brings relief to millions of restless people. The poet was correct when he wrote:

> Precious Name; Oh, how sweet:
> Hope of earth, and joy of Heaven.

# EMMANUEL

(MATTHEW 1:23)

During the reign of Ahaz in Judah, the nation was threatened by invasion and internal dissension, and it was at that time God commissioned Isaiah to deliver a message to the beleaguered monarch. The Lord's promise to help His people was expressed in a fascinating manner. The prophet said, "Therefore the Lord himself shall give you a sign; Behold, a virgin shall conceive, and bear a son, and shall call his name Immanuel" (Isa. 7:14). Centuries later, Matthew wrote concerning the birth of the Savior, "Now all this was done, that it might be fulfilled which was spoken of the Lord by the prophet, saying, Behold a virgin shall be with child, and shall bring forth a son, and they shall call his name Emmanuel, which being interpreted is, God with us" (Matt. 1:22-23).

*A great announcement . . . "God for us"*

Paul expressed generations of history and faith when he wrote: "What shall we then say to these things? If God be for us, who can be against us?" (Rom. 8:31). Doubtless, that was the predominant thought in the mind of Ahaz when he considered the dangers which threatened to destroy his kingdom. The opposing enemy had several powerful allies against whom it was almost impossible to prevail. Nevertheless, the idea of having the Almighty as a Helper and Friend had encouraged Israel throughout the centuries. God had accompanied His people during the many years of wilderness wanderings, and if He would help once again, no enemy could prevail against His people. The king's thoughts were limited to the urgent need of his situation. When Isaiah delivered his message, it became evident that God's vision was infinitely wider in scope; he thought of a far reaching world. Jehovah was the *God of the impossible*! A virgin would conceive, and from her womb would come a Deliverer to help all nations. At one time in the history of Israel, the concept of having God as an ally was the most marvelous privilege afforded to the Hebrews.

*A gracious achievement . . . "God with us"*

This was not a new doctrine in Israel. The Almighty had always been close to His people, and that was proved when He instructed Moses to erect a tabernacle in which the Lord could dwell among the tribes. The cloud by day, and the fire by night indicated His presence would be permanent. Moses, the revered leader, was God's channel of communication with them. Yet, the most brilliant thinkers in the nation could not have appreciated the magnitude of the promise given through Isaiah. That a virgin should conceive and bear a son was apparently beyond the realms of possibility. They could understand how God dwelled in a house constructed of materials, but to believe that the great Creator—their God, their Jehovah—would dwell in the body of a new-born child was unimaginable. Later, when Jesus claimed that such had been the case, the Jews became angry and accused him of blasphemy. They failed to understand Paul's message: "Great is the mystery of godliness: God was manifest in the flesh, justified in the Spirit, seen of angels, preached unto the Gentiles, believed on in the world, received up into glory" (1 Tim. 3:16).

*A glorious attainment . . . "God in us"*

Sometimes the message and methods of God are almost incomprehensible. When the Savior ascended into heaven, His enemies were probably delighted by the prospect of never having to be troubled again by the Man from Nazareth. They had no knowledge of God's plans for those who trusted in Christ. Paul wrote, "that Christ may dwell in your hearts by faith" (Eph. 3:17) and John also declared: "If we love one another, *God dwelleth in us,* and his love is perfected in us" (1 John 4:12). That the eternal God planned to live in the redeemed souls of sinners was something beyond comprehension, and yet this inestimable happiness became the experience of innumerable Christians. God is no longer the Occupier of distant planets nor the veiled mystery enshrined in an ornate temple. He now looks through the compassionate eyes of His children, shares the secret council-chambers of their minds, and is gradually transforming His family into His own likeness. Most of the followers of Christ may never be given the privilege of living in a presidential palace, but every day they may enjoy unending fellowship with their Redeemer. It is wonderful to know the Lord is *for* and *with* and, best of all, *within* His people. They enjoy excellent company!

# THE CARPENTER'S SON

(MATTHEW 13:55; LUKE 4:22)

It is thought that when Joseph died, Jesus became the supervisor of the carpenter's shop in Nazareth. He was known as "the carpenter's son" and, eventually, the name became a stigma. The citizens thought it ludicrous to associate a workman with royalty! They asked: "How could any laborer who took days to repair a wagon claim that he had created worlds in moments?" There is reason to believe that Christ's work was satisfactory, His prices fair, and His customer-relations superb. Even when clients disliked His teaching, they refrained from taking their business elsewhere. No other could equal the excellence of Him who was expert in handling *ordinary wagons* and *orbiting worlds!* The Lord was excellent at mending things and preached with His hands long before He addressed the multitudes in Galilee.

*The carpenter's Son in the shop*

Probably this was one of the most intriguing periods in the life of the Savior. When Jesus was twelve years old, His parents took Him to their home in Nazareth. When the Lord was thirty years of age, He attended meetings in the Jordan Valley and was baptized by John. Nothing is known of the intervening period in Nazareth. Maybe the Lord attended the school of the local rabbi, but since Joseph and Mary were peasants, it is more than likely that Jesus, at a very early age, joined Joseph in the family business. Many questions might be asked of that period in His life. At the age of twelve He was aware of His special relationship with Jehovah (see Luke 2:49), but to what extent that knowledge influenced His life it is hard to comprehend. When Jesus handled the timber in the shop, was He aware that He had made the trees from which it came? The Boy was an attentive student, but was He aware He had designed the universe and already knew far more than the man who taught the skills of carpentry? As the Lord grew older, did Satan ever use antagonistic customers in an endeavor to irritate the Savior? What happened when greedy customers argued about the fair prices charged by Jesus? The carpenter's shop might have been a battleground where Jesus was constantly tempted.

*The carpenter's Son in the synagogue*

It was the Sabbath day, but the people in the synagogue were apprehensive. One of their citizens had returned to Nazareth, and every person was speculating regarding the outcome of His visit. Rumor said that Jesus had become a great faith-healer, but some of the citizens thought the reports were exaggerations, the product of overwrought minds. That Sabbath would either endorse or destroy what had been said. As the service proceeded, the critical congregation became offended by His presence and power, asking, "Whence hath this man this wisdom, and these mighty works? Is not this the carpenter's son?" (Matt. 13:55). Their attempt to kill the Lord was foiled when "he passing through the midst of them, went his way" (Luke 4:30). Those people were very foolish. Did it really matter whose son the Teacher might be? Miracles endorsed His teaching, while healed men and women provided evidence that God had honored and used one of their citizens. The fact that He had been a carpenter might have suggested wonderful truths to their minds.

*The carpenter's Son in the Scriptures*

(1) *A carpenter can re-make things.* Articles of furniture damaged almost beyond repair can be transformed by the efforts of a master-workman. Things which ordinarily would be rejected may once again occupy a place in a world of usefulness. That identical truth was expressed by the Lord when He said, "I will restore to you the years that the locust hath eaten" (Joel 2:25). (2) *A carpenter can strengthen things.* When a chair or a wagon cannot carry its load and is in danger of collapsing, the skill of the workman enables it to do what is expected from it. That same truth was expressed by God in Isaiah 41:10. (3) *A carpenter builds things.* His skill is used in the construction of homes, churches, and other necessary edifices. He is able to read blueprints and bring into being that which was planned from the beginning! Evidently, the Great Carpenter had this in mind when He said to Peter, "I will build my church, and the gates of hell shall not prevail against it" (see Matt. 16:18).

# THE BUILDER

(MATTHEW 16:18)

It is not difficult to understand why people called God "The Supreme Architect." He was the Master-builder who supplied Moses with the intricate designs of the tabernacle and insisted that everything be done according to His masterplan. Jehovah was always interested in bringing things into being, as it is written: "In the beginning God created the heaven and the earth" (Gen. 1:1). It was to be expected that John would attribute identical characteristics to Christ. The apostle wrote, "All things were made by him [The Word — Jesus]; and without him was not anything made that was made" (John 1:3). Throughout the New Testament, Christ is represented as a builder and certain things become obvious when the Scriptures are examined.

*The masterplan . . . to suggest*

A builder who operates without a plan encounters problems. His employees have nothing to study, with the result that the building will be disappointing and confusing. When God created the human body, He considered what He was about to do. Afterward David said, "I will praise thee; for I am fearfully and wonderfully made: marvellous are thy works; and that my soul knoweth right well" (Ps. 139:14). Paul evidently believed that his Lord had a preconceived plan "to make in himself of twain one new man" (Eph. 2:15). Furthermore, the apostle indicated that this plan had existed from eternal ages. He wrote, "He hath chosen us in him before the foundation of the world, that we should be holy and without blame before him in love" (Eph. 1:4). Paul described this masterplan, which remained unrevealed and unexplained throughout the ages and "which in other ages was not made known unto the sons of men, as it is now revealed unto his holy apostles and prophets by the Spirit" (Eph. 3:5). God's plan was very explicit, nothing was left to chance. When the Son of God came to earth, He came to put into operation that which had been decided in the eternal counsels of God. Peter said of the Lord, "Him, being delivered by *the determinate counsel and foreknowledge of God,* ye have taken, and by wicked hands have crucified and slain" (Acts 2:23).

*The materials . . . supplied*

Plans are useless unless materials are forthcoming by which they can be put into operation. Paul believed that God desired all racial strife to cease; that men should live harmoniously, and that all nations should be united in the fellowship of the family of God. Throughout centuries of human history, this appeared to be an impossibility, but the death and resurrection of Jesus performed miracles! Jesus announced to Peter His intention to build His Church, and later the apostle referred to the Christians as "lively [living] stones built into a spiritual house" (see 1 Peter 2:5). Paul wrote to the Ephesian church, "In whom ye also are builded together for an habitation of God through the Spirit" (Eph. 2:22). Evidently, men were filled with sinful blemishes and unfit for a place in God's temple. Christ came to reclaim, cleanse, and beautify lost stones and to incorporate them into His Church. Without His intervention, guilty people would have been rejected eternally.

*The men . . . to serve*

Prior to the Lord's ascension to heaven, He said to the disciples, "In my Father's house are many mansions: if it were not so, I would have told you. I go to prepare a place for you" (John 14:2). That is the city in which Christ and His bride will reside forever. It is called the "New Jerusalem" (see Rev. 21:9-27). Until we enter that perfect place, the Lord sent the Holy Spirit to be the divine Overseer of the erection of *the church on earth.* Obviously, as with any building, workmen are necessary, and one of the greatest privileges ever given to men and women is that of helping in the erection of the true Church of Christ. For example, Paul described himself as "a wise masterbuilder" (1 Cor. 3:10) and indicated that others were also helping in the work of construction. The Lord Jesus Christ is building an edifice which will defy the ravages of time; it will last throughout eternity. Compared with the work of redemption, even the creation of the universe fades into insignificance. S. J. Stone was correct when he wrote:

> The Church's one foundation
> Is Jesus Christ her Lord.
> She is His new creation
> By water and the Word:
> From Heaven He came and sought her
> To be His holy Bride,
> With His own blood He bought her,
> And for her life, He died.

# JESUS OF NAZARETH

(MATTHEW 21:11)

The New Testament mentions other men whose name was Jesus, but only One was called *Jesus of Nazareth.* When He entered triumphantly into Jerusalem, the excited crowds exclaimed: "This is Jesus, the prophet of Nazareth in Galilee." Throughout His unprecedented ministry, Jesus was more than a Preacher—He was a Prophet. He was neither a glamorous man who belonged to Herod's family nor a distinguished member of the nation's powerful Sanhedrin. He was a Carpenter whose hands were often soiled by the work of the day. He was neither a product of Hebrew learning, nor a graduate from the famous theological school of Gamaliel. As far as is known, the Lord never attended any school. The news of His ability to heal the sick aroused excitement in Jerusalem, but when the expected miracles were not forthcoming, the crowd decreased in size, and the city was disturbed by demands for His crucifixion. The people said He was *a prophet* from Nazareth in Galilee. Peter said He was the *Prince of Life* (Acts 3:15), but God said, "This is *my beloved Son,* in whom I am well pleased" (Matt. 17:5).

*The name of shame . . . John 1:45-46*

"Philip findeth Nathanael, and saith unto him, We have found him, of whom Moses in the law, and the prophets, did write, Jesus of Nazareth, the son of Joseph. And Nathanael said unto him, Can any good thing come out of Nazareth?" That statement reflected the attitude of the nation. The town's population had a large contingent of semi-pagans whose rough dialect contrasted with the language of the Jews. Nazareth was never mentioned in the Old Testament, but during the days of the Maccabees, it acquired an evil reputation and was despised by the Hebrews. Matthew said that Joseph brought Jesus to Nazareth "that it might be fulfilled which was spoken by the prophets, He shall be called a Nazarene." Even the Jews who resided in the city exhibited the detestable characteristics of the half-heathen population, for even on their Sabbath Day, they tried to murder the Savior (see Matt. 2:23 and Luke 4:28-29). It was significant that when Nicodemus tried to defend the Lord, the members of the Sanhedrin replied: "Art thou also of Galilee? Search, and look, for out of Galilee ariseth no prophet" (John 7:52). Nazareth, so it was claimed, was the home of everything detestable, but Jesus never avoided being among its unlovely citizens.

*The name of blame . . . John 19:19*

"And Pilate wrote a title, and put it on the cross. And the writing was, JESUS, OF NAZARETH, THE KING OF THE JEWS." There is reason to believe Pilate carefully chose the words of that inscription. He could have been content with, ''This is the King of the Jews,'' or even ''This is Jesus, the King of the Jews.'' The inclusion of the word *Nazareth* implied the irony of the situation; it expressed the resentment of the governor. Israel's ''King'' had ascended from the most despised part of the land, and the title placed on the cross was an insult to the people responsible for the execution. It expressed indignity and humiliation and reflected their rejection of the claims made throughout the Lord's ministry. ''He came unto his own, and his own received him not'' (John 1:11). Jesus was blamed for claiming equality with God; for breaking the law; for being an associate of Beelzebub, the chief of devils, and for threatening to destroy the temple (see Matt. 26:61). These accusations led to His indictment and subsequent death.

*The name of fame. . . Acts 10:38*

It is important to remember that this name, which was used by the preachers and leaders of the church, is mentioned seven times in the Acts of the Apostles, and supplies evidence that what men rejected, God signally honored. Peter claimed that Jesus of Nazareth was *approved of God* (Acts 2:22), involved in *the healing of the cripple* (Acts 3:6), *raised from the dead by God* (Acts 4:10), and was *the Anointed One of God* (Acts 10:38). ''The head that once was crowned with thorns is crowned with glory now.'' As with other titles given to the Lord, Jesus of Nazareth linked the ignominy and shame of Nazareth with the inspiration and splendor of heaven. It provided evidence that the whitest lilies sometimes emerge from the dirtiest ponds!

# THAT JUST MAN

(MATTHEW 27:19)

The Greek word *dikaio,* which has been translated "just", is interesting; its derivatives are used throughout the New Testament to express various ideas. It was used to indicate a righteous person without bias, prejudice, and partiality. It indicated the worthiness expected from a judge and reflected excellence of character, unbiased consideration, and unquestioned integrity. This was one of the names given to the Savior, and when considered in its various settings, it becomes intriguing.

*Revealed in a dream (Matt. 27:19)*

"When he [Pilate] was set down on the judgment seat, his wife sent unto him, saying, Have thou nothing to do with *that just man:* for I have suffered many things this day in a dream because of him." Wordsworth remarks: "In the whole history of the Passion of Christ, no one pleads for him but a woman, the wife of a heathen governor, the deputy of the emperor of the world" *(The Pulpit Commentary, Matthew,* Vol. Two, p. 585). It is thought that this woman was a convert to Judaism and that she was acquainted with Jewish affairs. Perhaps she had conversed with her husband about the Man whose presence thrilled the common people. It is certain that on the morning when Pilate went out to preside at the trial of Jesus, his wife had a very vivid dream. No one knows what she saw and heard, but the message sent later to Pilate indicated admiration for the accused Carpenter. She believed Jesus to be a *just Man,* incapable of committing a crime.

*Remembered in a dilemma (Matt. 27:24)*

Pilate was in great trouble; the crowd was clamoring for a victim. Matthew wrote, "When Pilate saw that he could prevail nothing, but that rather a tumult was made, he took water, and washed his hands before the multitude, saying, I am innocent of the blood of *this just person:* see ye to it." His wife's description of the Accused echoed through his mind; had he granted her request, his soul might have been saved. Although he remained unaware of the importance of her statement, it was in actual fact the final attempt made by God to save the governor from eternal condemnation. The qualities Claudias saw in Jesus should have been present in her husband.

*Repeated in a discourse (Acts 3:14)*

The news of the healing of the cripple had electrified Jerusalem. Great numbers of people rushed to the sanctuary to hear more of the startling event. "And when Peter saw it, he answered unto the people, Ye men of Israel, why marvel ye at this? or why look ye so earnestly on us, as though by our own power or holiness we had made this man to walk? The God of. . . our fathers, hath glorified his Son Jesus; whom ye delivered up. . . . But ye denied the Holy One and *the Just,* and desired a murderer to be granted unto you; and killed the Prince of life, whom God hath raised from the dead; whereof we are witnesses" (Acts 3:12-15). Peter deliberately reminded the Jews of their dastardly deed and in so doing contrasted *the Just Savior* with *the unjust Barabbas.* Jesus represented everything good, the robber exhibited everything evil.

*Recognized in a document (Rom. 3:26)*

During the centuries, every rabbi in Israel taught that sinners could not be justified before God. The continuing performance of good deeds could influence the Almighty and at least gain for the individual a degree of merit before Jehovah. Then Paul announced that no human merit could bridge the gulf between God's holiness and man's sin. He affirmed that faith in Jesus alone can remove human guilt and bring unending peace to the human conscience. That seems unfair. Why should sinners receive in a moment that for which others had worked throughout a lifetime? How then could God be just if He sanctioned justification? The apostle's thesis on this subject is contained in the letter sent to the church in Rome. God the Father and His Son were both *Just;* our heavenly Father sacrificed His Son to make salvation possible; the Lord Jesus voluntarily liquidated the debt of sin. No charge of injustice can be brought against the Savior, because He has satisfied every requirement of righteousness. There is no longer need to earn salvation; it is the "unspeakable gift of God."

# THE SON OF GOD

(MARK 1:1)

Throughout the history of the Church, the name "Son of God" has been the target of critics. Within the early assemblies of Christians, arguments continued. Therefore, in order to give guidance to confused members, church councils were convened. It was affirmed that if Jesus were *the Son* of God, He was less than the Father. If He were the Son, He had a beginning! Therefore, it was taught that God existed before "the Son," and consequently was greater than He. People ignored the fact that any son may be greater than his father. A child may have more education, money, ability, and experience than his father ever possessed. From many viewpoints, a son may be greater than his father.

A man is called "a son," not because he is less than his father but rather to show he is of the same essence, that he belongs to the same family, that he has the same blood. Jesus, the Word, was in the beginning with God, and He *was* God (see John 1:1). Then the Almighty did something which was almost inconceivable. He decided to embark on a mission of mercy and, to make it possible, created a body! "Wherefore, when he cometh into the world, he saith. . .a body hast thou prepared me" (Heb. 10:5). Isaiah predicted that *a child* would be born, but *the Son* would be given (Isa. 9:6). Jehovah was manifesting Himself in a new way, and the One who began life as a baby became known as the *only begotten Son of God.*

*The Son of God. . .the glory of His person*

Referring to the Savior, the writer to the Hebrews said: "Who being the brightness of his glory, and the express image of his person, and upholding all things by the word of his power, when he had by himself purged our sins, sat down on the right hand of the Majesty on high" (Heb. 1:3). The disciples never forgot the moment when the effulgence of Christ's nature broke through the frail barrier of flesh, and the eternal glories became visible to mortal men (see Matt. 17:2 and 2 Peter 1:16). The Lord's inherent beauty transcended everything ever known; He was indeed the fairest among ten thousand, and the altogether lovely (Song of Sol. 5:16).

*The Son of God. . .the graciousness of His privilege*

The high priest of Israel was permitted to enter into the Holy of Holies once every year. That event took place on the Day of Atonement, when the blood of the offering was sprinkled upon and before the mercy seat. Afterward, when the priest withdrew, intimate fellowship with God remained unreachable for another twelve months. When the Savior began His ministry in heaven, He remained there. A son may enter into the presence of his father at any time; access to the home is not limited. This was the privilege given exclusively to Christ; He was not a stranger in heaven. It might be truthful to say that He was far more at home there than He ever was on earth.

*The Son of God . . . the greatness of His power*

A trusted son generally becomes the executor or administrator of his father's last will and testament. If it be so desired, the son may assume responsibilities during the parent's lifetime. God is immortal, He will never die. Paul wrote about the Lord, "... that in all things he might have the preeminence. For it pleased the Father that in him should all fullness dwell" (Col. 1:18-19).

*The Son of God . . . the gratification of His pleasure*

Any son who is precious in the sight of his father may introduce his friends at any time. The intimacy between parent and child is the guarantee of acceptance for a stranger. That was precisely what Paul meant when he wrote: "He hath made us accepted in the beloved" (Eph. 1:6). It is thrilling to know that this favor will be extended throughout eternity. Paul stated, "That in the ages to come he might shew the exceeding riches of his grace in his kindness toward us through Christ Jesus" (Eph. 2:7). The Lord was called both "The Son of God," and "The Son of Man." The first name represents the heavenward side of the link that eternally unites us with Christ, who loved us and gave himself for us (see Gal. 2:20).

# THE HOLY ONE OF GOD

(Mark 1:24)

Most of the names given to Christ are sources of inspiration which supply strength to the weak, hope for the despondent, and comfort to those who mourn. They were given by prophets or by people whom Christ had changed and transformed. They range from lofty revelations of His magnificence to the humblest of occupations where daily work soiled the Carpenter's hands. One name was different. It still sends chills through the soul and apprehension through the mind. It was the name given by demons who were terrified by Christ's presence and fearful of their immediate future. One of the evil spirits which enslaved the worshiper in the synagogue looked at Jesus and said, "I know thee who thou art, the Holy One of God."

*How significant*

Expectancy filled the synagogue; people who were normally bored were excited; an important visitor was in the congregation. The rabbi, as he usually did with strangers, would surely ask Jesus to address the congregation. They were not disappointed; the expected invitation was given, and every person present waited in eager expectation. Mark, describing the occasion, wrote: "And they went into Capernaum; and straightway on the sabbath day he entered into the synagogue, and taught" (Mark 1:21). Then came the ominous interruption, "And there was in their synagogue a man with an unclean spirit; and he cried out" (v. 23). Every worshiper frowned—this was sacrilege; why did not the fellow hold his peace? The sanctuary was not a place for brawling! Surely, an usher or official would either silence the offender or escort him to the street. "What have we to do with thee, thou Jesus of Nazareth. Art thou come to destroy us?" The men stared at the demoniac and suddenly the cry became more personalized: "I know thee who thou art, the Holy One of God" (v. 24). The question may be asked, "From where did such knowledge come?" The local people saw only a carpenter from Nazareth, but the demons possessed knowledge which went back to the commencement of time.

*How sustained*

This startling confession, arising from evil spirits, was not a "once in a lifetime" experience. The statement was the continuing testimony of demons. It remains a startling fact that whereas men continued to criticize the Lord, evil spirits never denied the deity of the Savior. They had been present from the beginning and unfortunately had taken part in the insurrection instigated by Lucifer. They joined the rebellion in heaven and were banished from the presence of the Almighty. We may never know the extent of the animosity and rebellion which continued to dominate Satan's associates, but it is undeniable that never on any occasion did demons deny the Lordship of Christ. Luke also mentioned how fraudulent men tried to expel an evil spirit, but the possessed man answered, "Jesus I know, and Paul I know; but who are ye?" (Acts 19:13-16). The imposters fled naked and wounded, and as a result, "the name of the Lord Jesus was magnified" (Acts 19:17). Sometimes demons are wiser than men! Although Jesus appeared as a man, nothing destroyed the demonic assurance that He was the holy Son of God.

*How sad*

Language cannot describe the eternal tragedy of being banished from God. That, apparently, is something beyond the limits of human comprehension. The evil spirits not only witnessed the amazing exploits of God and His Son; they even confessed, however reluctantly, that Jesus was divine. Nevertheless, they remained without hope of salvation. The sentence of death passed upon them could not be changed. Their fear of being alone "in the deep" (Luke 8:31) filled them with dread. They had made their decision earlier in time and, unfortunately, were following a path which led inevitably to destruction. The writer to the Hebrews expressed this tragic truth when he asked the unanswerable question: "How shall we escape if we neglect so great salvation?" (Heb. 2:3).

# THE SON OF MARY

(MARK 6:3)

The Son of Mary was the most natural name ever given to the Savior. "When [Joseph] heard that Archelaus did reign. . .in the room of his father Herod, he was afraid to go thither: notwithstanding, being warned of God in a dream, he turned aside into the parts of Galilee: And he came and dwelt in a city called Nazareth: that it might be fulfilled which was spoken by the prophets, He shall be called a Nazarene" (Matt. 2:22-23). Nazareth was only a small town, and the arrival of a new family would be known to all its citizens. When Joseph commenced business as a carpenter, customers were attracted from every section of the community, and many of them saw Mary with her Child. Jesus grew up in those surroundings and doubtless became a regular worshiper in the local synagogue. It was therefore understandable that when disdain and anger filled the disrespectful congregation, many of whom asked, "Is not this the carpenter, the son of Mary, the brother of James, and Joses? and of Judah, and Simon? and are not his sisters here with us? And they were offended at him" (Mark 6:3).

*The unique disclosure . . . "She was . . . with child of the Holy Ghost"*

The citizens of Nazareth were unaware that, basically, Mary was *not* the mother of Jesus. She was the chosen instrument through whom the Son of God entered the world. Had she been His mother, she would have—with Joseph— transmitted to her Baby, a nature corrupted by sin. Within the sacred precincts of her womb, she protected and nourished the fetus of her Child, *but God supplied the seed.* That delightful maiden was chosen by God to carry the precious Baby to the time of His birth. She fed, protected, delivered, clothed, and certainly loved Him, but she never gave Him life! This was a fact unknown to the people among whom Christ lived.

*The unconsidered detail . . . "A virgin shall conceive"*

"Therefore the Lord himself shall give you a sign; behold a virgin shall conceive, and bear a son, and shall call his name Immanuel" (Isa. 7:14). A virgin is "a person, especially a young woman, who has never had sexual intercourse" (*The Reader's Digest Great Encyclopedic Dictionary*). Had the scribes and Pharisees considered the statement made by their prophet, they would have known that young women sacrificed their virginity to make possible the birth of their first child. Had the citizens of Nazareth understood their Scriptures, they would have known that the birth of the Messiah necessitated a miracle. Matthew understood this fact and, in describing the incarnation, wrote: "Now all this was done, that it might be fulfilled which was spoken of the Lord by the prophet, . . . Behold, a virgin shall be with child, and shall bring forth a son, and they shall call his name Emmanuel, which being interpreted is, God with us'' (Matt. 1:22-23).

*The unsurpassed discernment . . . ''Mary . . . pondered these things''*

''But Mary was keeping, within herself, all these things [sayings] weighing and pondering them in her heart'' (Luke 2:19) *(The Amplified New Testament). The New English Bible* translates the verse: ''But Mary treasured up all these things and pondered over them.'' That delightful lady grew accustomed to hearing her neighbors referring to Jesus as her Son, but within her soul, she knew that He was the Son of God. Possibly she was reluctant to describe the intimate details of her pregnancy — except to her friend, Dr. Luke. The growth of her faith became apparent when, at the wedding in Cana, she instructed the servants, ''Whatsoever he saith unto you, do it'' (John 2:5). As far as is known, Jesus, at that time, had not performed any public miracles, but His mother knew He could, even before He did.

*The unfortunate doubting . . . ''He is beside himself''*

''And when his friends [kinsmen] heard of it, they went out to lay hold on him: for they said, He is beside himself'' (Mark 3:21). It is not possible to be sure whether or not doubt filled Mary's mind. The astonishing statements attributed to Jesus and the rising tide of animosity resulting from His claims certainly influenced His family. Their subsequent attempt to remove Jesus from the crowds supply food for thought. Evidently, they were afraid that He was in danger of becoming mentally deranged. It is not difficult for us to understand and, perhaps, excuse their lack of faith. Evidently, Mary was worried beyond measure, but maybe her faith shone brightest in the dark. Even though she knew He was really God's Son, she loved Him just as much as though He had been her own.

# THE PREACHER

(LUKE 4:18-19)

During the history of the human race, people have listened to many preachers. Some were refined graduates from academic institutions; others were ordinary men from inauspicious occupations. Solomon, who was more a poet than a preacher, excelled with his wisdom and pen. Amos was a dresser of trees; he was rough, rugged, and outspoken. Simon and his brethren were fishermen from Galilee. Matthew, a bookkeeper, was employed as a government tax collector. Luke was a physician who preached more with his hands than with words. Paul was trained in the school of Gamaliel. Martin Luther was a monk; William Carey, a shoemaker; David Livingstone, a young, self-taught boy from a poor home in Scotland. These became men of renown, preachers from whom millions of people heard the gospel.

Unlike some of His servants, Jesus never swayed people with mere rhetoric. He never used an excessive vocabulary, and listeners never needed to consult a dictionary to ascertain the meaning of His words. His speech was so simple children understood His message. Yet, it was so profound, and sincere that scholars have never ridiculed His teachings. He was a master at the art of story telling and was never short of subject matter. He spoke about birds and flowers, fishing, sheep, robbers, and ordinary items of daily life. His gracious words made drab things lovely; His gentle touch made sick people well; His glorious gospel turned sinners into saints. He was the greatest of all preachers.

*The Preacher's communion . . . prayer preceded preaching*

"And in the morning, rising up a great while before day, he went out, and departed into a solitary place, and there prayed" (Mark 1:35). Even the Lord needed the sustaining strength obtained only through communion with His Father, for each day brought new problems. To meet demands made upon Him, Jesus communed with God before He looked at His congregation. Wise ministers emulate His example.

*The Preacher's conviction . . . He was sure of His message*

The Lord's sermons were never ambiguous. He believed implicitly in the Word of God, which was the basis of all He uttered. His statements were challenging, His exposition of truth convincing, and His commitment to evangelism unfaltering. Christ knew the urgency of the situation and continually endeavored to bring people to repentance.

*The Preacher's carefulness . . . His language was easily understood*

The children who listened to the Savior understood what was being said. His illustrations were always related to commonplace events and circumstances. Probably the longest word Jesus ever used was *whosoever.* It would have been foolish to utter words unknown to His audience. Preachers who become slaves to excessive verbiage have much to learn.

*The Preacher's consecration . . . He was full of the Holy Spirit*

The Bible never says that Jesus was *filled* with the Spirit; He was always *full*. It is not possible to fill a vessel that is already overflowing! Moment by moment, day after day, Jesus was energized by the power of God, and that was the secret of His remarkable ministry.

*The Preacher's courage . . . He never compromised His message*

There were times of danger during the Lord's ministry. Other men would have avoided conflict with adversaries. The scribes and Pharisees were antagonistic; the Sadducees disapproved of His doctrines and tried to murder the Savior. Yet, undaunted and unafraid, Jesus continued His ministry and never failed to deliver His message.

*The Preacher's confidence . . . He knew He would succeed*

The Lord was convinced that in spite of apparent setbacks, the purposes of God would be achieved; the gates of hell would not prevail against His Church (see Matt. 16:18). Despair never undermined His faith. He knew that although evil might win occasional battles, the final triumph belonged to God. It may be impossible for Christians to equal the Lord's excellence, but they should never cease trying.

Lord, speak to me that I may speak  
In living echoes of Thy tone;  
As Thou hast sought, so let me seek,  
Thy erring children, lost and lone.

# A FRIEND OF PUBLICANS AND SINNERS

(LUKE 7:34)

The term "a friend," is possibly the warmest and most attractive phrase in any language. It denotes intimacy, love, trust, and dependability. There may be a great difference between a friend and an associate in a financial enterprise. A business relationship may be the product of necessity; it may not reflect affection between the people involved. True friendship is the result of love, understanding, and concern, so that, although unpleasant circumstances may occasionally hurt the relationship, they never destroy that which is indestructible. The friendship which existed between David and Jonathan exhibited characteristics which are admired by all people. Friendship is a bridge which spans the gulf between riches and poverty, education and illiteracy. It recognizes no racial barriers and represents the only true hope for world peace.

PROPOSITION 1 . . . *True Friends love each other's company*

The life-style of Jesus contrasted completely with that of the Pharisees. Their strange and sometimes hypocritical doctrines demanded separation from sinners. They considered it undesirable for people from a lower social order to be permitted to attend feasts or functions to which they had been invited. On the other hand, Jesus mingled with all kinds of people and found pleasure in preaching to outcasts. His actions invited criticism, and His enemies seized every opportunity to denounce His behavior. It became increasingly evident that sinners and the Savior welcomed each other's company. He enjoyed telling them about the good news of salvation, and they appreciated listening to the greatest Preacher they had ever heard.

PROPOSITION 2 . . . *True Friends share each other's problems*

The impoverished people of Palestine had many problems. They were economically poor, many were suffering from a variety of diseases, and all were oppressed by circumstances beyond their control. Unfortunately, advice or help received from the religious leaders was often expensive; the priests did not work for nothing! Medical science was not then as it is now; consequently, many sufferers had no hope of recovering their health. Lepers were considered to be dead even before they died! The darkness in which these people existed seemed to be impenetrable and then the Sun of Righteousness suddenly arose with healing in His wings (see Mal. 4:2). It was no cause for amazement when "the common people heard Jesus gladly;" He brought them deliverance beyond the limits of comprehension. He not only understood their predicament, He obviously appreciated their problems.

PROPOSITION 3 . . . *True Friends protect each other's interests*

Jesus' protecting others' interests became evident during the supper in the home of Simon the Pharisee. When a woman of ill repute made her appearance and anointed the feet of Jesus, the host said, "This man, if he were a prophet, would have known who and what manner of woman this is that toucheth him: for she is a sinner" (Luke 7:39). The response given by Jesus was exceedingly gracious, and the world now admires the kindness and affection with which He pled the woman's case. Jesus was not prepared to hear derogatory remarks concerning a penitent soul who had expressed love for the Lord. He was on her side and evidently she was on His.

PROPOSITION 4 . . . *True Friends rejoice in each other's success*

When it became obvious that David would become the king of Israel, Jonathan was filled with ecstasy. Jealousy had no place within his soul. As a contrast to this attitude, David wept when he realized his best friend would be denied his heritage. Either man would have died for the other. Jonathan would have gladly placed the crown on David's head, and David would have been thrilled to transfer it back to the head of his dearest friend. When these same attributes were recognized in the relationship between Christ and His followers, it became easy to understand why He was called "the Friend of publicans and sinners." When the seventy disciples returned to testify concerning their unprecedented triumphs, "in that hour, Jesus rejoiced in spirit, and said, I thank thee, O Father, Lord of heaven and earth, that thou hast hid these things from the wise and prudent, and hast revealed them unto babes . . ." (Luke 10:21). He rejoiced in their happiness.

I've found a Friend, Oh, such a Friend:<br>
So kind and true and tender.<br>
So wise a Counsellor and Guide,<br>
So mighty a Defender.<br>
From Him, Who loves me now so well,<br>
What power my soul can sever?<br>
Shall life? or death? or earth? or hell?<br>
No! I am His forever.

# THE GALILEAN

(LUKE 23:6)

Galilee was a scenic center in Israel, but it remained one of the nation's most unpopular places. Orthodox Jews admired the countryside but detested its inhabitants. Far back in history, Solomon gave to Hiram twenty unimportant towns (1 Kings 9:11), but they were all in Galilee. He gave away what he did not desire. The area became known as *Galilee of the nations,* indicating the population was composed of numerous nationalities (Isa. 9:1). Many of the inhabitants were captured during the Assyrian wars, and the few Jews who remained were taken by Simon Maccabaeus to Judea. Later, many of these returned, so that the district once again became thickly populated. Nevertheless, old traditions did not die overnight, and many Jews continued to look with disdain upon the territory. They taught that no prophet of God could arise in Galilee with the result that it became a continuing source of annoyance when Jesus spent most of His time in Capernaum and adjacent cities.

*How suggestive . . . God may be found in the most unlikely place*

"The people of Galilee were specially blamed for neglecting the study of their language, charged with errors in grammar and with absurd malpronunciation, sometimes leading to ridiculous mistakes. Thus there was general contempt in Rabbinic circles for all that was Galilean. The people were easily recognized by their dialect, and tone, as was seen by the detection of Peter as one of Christ's disciples . . . (see Mark 14:70)" *(Unger's Bible Dictionary,* p. 387). That the Messiah or anything good should come from Galilee was unacceptable to the Jewish leaders. "Of a truth this is the Prophet. Others said, this is the Christ. But some said, Shall Christ come out of Galilee?" (John 7:40-41).

*How stupid . . . to permit bigotry is to reject truth*

When the Lord was accused before Pilate, the Jewish leaders said, "He stirreth up the people, teaching throughout all Jewry, beginning from Galilee to this place. When Pilate heard of Galilee, he asked whether the man [Jesus] were a Galilean" (Luke 23:5-6). Evidently, the stigma of that name was associated with the Savior, so that His chances of release diminished when the presiding judge discovered that Jesus had associations with the despised people of the nation. Unfortunately, this characteristic continued through the history of the church. Flavius Claudius Julianus, the Roman Emperor from A.D. 361 to A.D. 363, renounced Christianity and attempted to restore paganism. He called Christ "the Galilean God." He also made a law requiring that all Christians should be called by no other name, hoping thereby to abolish the name Christian. It is said that he died fighting against the followers of Jesus and that as he caught in his hand the blood coming from a wound in his side, he threw it toward heaven, saying, "Thou hast conquered, O Galilean!" Unfortunately, many other unbelievers made the same mistake. A warped and closed mind never learns anything.

*How sublime . . . God can use anyone who is willing to serve Him*

When Peter and the other disciples preached on the day of Pentecost, the people "were all amazed and marvelled, saying one to another, Behold, are not all these which speak Galileans? And how hear we every man in our own tongue, wherein we were born?" (Acts 2:7-8). That the Spirit of God should use the detested men from Galilee was probably the greatest surprise ever to confront the critical Jews. It indicated God was no respecter of persons and that lineage and ancestry could never compete with the attractiveness of clean, surrendered lives. It has been claimed that out of the dirtiest ponds emerge the whitest lilies. This was apparent when men from the despised area of Galilee, eventually changed the world. Education can be one of the greatest assets of the Christian, but it is not an absolute prerequisite to blessing. The color of a man's skin and the type of accent with which he speaks may appear to be strange, but God "looketh upon the heart," and history attests the glorious fact that people of all races have faithfully served the Lord. There is reason to believe that when the kingdom of Christ is finally established, it will be impossible to find Germans, British, Russians, Jews, Gentiles among the citizens of the celestial city, for all men will have become brothers.

# THE WORD OF GOD

(JOHN 1:1; REVELATION 19:13)

The apostle John was a seer, a mystic, a visionary. It is intriguing that of all the New Testament authors he alone called Jesus "The Word." He did so in his Gospel (John 1:1 and 1:14). He repeated this in the Epistles which he addressed to his friends (1 John 5:7), and he did it again in the Book of Revelation (Rev. 19:13). Evidently, it was his favorite name for the Master. Why was this so? Words are vehicles of thought. A man may speak or write them, and if he is able to speak the deaf and dumb language, he may also use his hands to convey what cannot be heard. Unless a person expresses himself, his mind remains inscrutable. Similarly, God ordinarily would have remained beyond the comprehension of human beings. It became necessary for the Almighty to express Himself; in order to reveal Himself, He used the Word. Jesus became the channel of communication between God and human beings. "God, who at sundry times and in divers manners spake in time past unto the fathers by the prophets, hath in these last days spoken unto us by his Son" (Heb. 1:1-2).

*The Word in history . . . revealing*

"In the beginning was the Word, and the Word was with God, and the Word was God. . . .And the Word was made flesh, and dwelt among us, (and we beheld his glory)" (John 1:1 and 1:14). The apostle never changed his opinion about the Lord. Many years later he wrote: "That which was from the beginning, *which we have heard,* which we have seen with our eyes, which we have looked upon, and our hands have handled, of the Word of life. . . .That which we have seen and heard declare we unto you . . ." (1 John 1:1, 3). John taught that the Father and the Son were *one*; they were co-equal and co-existent. The apostle believed that when he listened to Jesus, he heard the voice and message of the Father. He was sure that when he gazed into the face of Jesus, he saw the face of God. Therefore, it was never difficult to believe what the Savior taught. Sometimes it was difficult to grasp the new revelations, but the veracity and reliability of the message were never questioned. Jesus was the expressed eloquence and wisdom of the Most High God.

*The Word in heaven . . . responding*

John watched the Lord's ascension into heaven, but there was never any real distance between the Savior and the apostle He left behind. The apostle recognized that Jesus had extended the scope of His amazing ministry. As He had represented God on earth, He was now representing His followers in heaven. As He had expressed

God's desires to men, He now was expressing human desires before the throne of grace. Jesus had become the great Attorney at the bar of divine justice; He was the High Priest of His people. "For Christ is not entered into the holy places made with hands, which are the figures of the true; but into heaven itself, now to appear in the presence of God for us" (Heb. 9:24). As Jesus was *God's* Word to us, He became *our* Word to God. There are times when we hardly know how to pray, but in those moments of frustration, the risen Lord becomes our spokesman before the throne of God—"He ever liveth to make intercession for us" (Heb. 7:25).

*The Word in the hereafter . . . returning*

"And I saw heaven opened, and behold a white horse, and he that sat upon him was called Faithful and True. . . . And he was clothed with a vesture dipped in blood: and his name is called The Word of God" (Rev. 19:11-13). John firmly believed Jesus would eventually return to establish His kingdom upon earth. God permitted His servant to see some of the amazing things to take place at the end of time, but the revelation was so great John had to use other definitions to express the amazement within his soul. For example, he referred to Jesus as "KING OF KINGS, AND LORD OF LORDS" (Rev. 19:16), but the old description remained. Even when Christ returns in celestial glory, He will still be *the Word*, and His raiment will remind viewers of His ordeal on the cross of Calvary. Throughout eternity Jesus will remain the expression of the Most High, and even His hands will remind saints of the price He paid for their redemption (see Zech. 13:6).

# THE LAMB OF GOD

(JOHN 1:29)

This is the most loved of all the names given to Christ. When John the Baptist said, "Behold the Lamb of God, which taketh away the sin of the world," his message reverberated around the world. Today, millions of Christians respond to that hallowed name; it represents all they consider to be precious. Long before time began, the Lamb of God was the focal point in God's plan for the future (Rev. 13:8). Throughout history, lambs were foremost in the thoughts of Israel, for they were sacrificed daily in the temple at Jerusalem. The nation could never forget that it was the blood of the lamb which prevented the destruction of their firstborn sons in Egypt (Exod. 12:5-7). When John was permitted to look into heaven, he recognized that the Lamb occupied the central place and was able to perform a deed beyond the capability of others (Rev. 5:4-7). It is thrilling to know that throughout endless ages, ten thousand times ten thousand, and thousands of thousands will unite to say, "Worthy is the Lamb that was slain" (Rev. 5:11-12). The Bible reminds readers that lambs were used for three purposes.

*The Lamb of sacrifice (Gen. 22:13)*

God always made provision whereby sinners could obtain forgiveness. The Lord was said to have been "the Lamb slain from before the foundation of the world." The lamb was the means of Israel's redemption, and throughout the New Testament Jesus was mentioned as the fulfillment of the doctrines enunciated by the prophets. Peter wrote, "Forasmuch as ye know that ye were not redeemed with corruptible things, as silver and gold. . . but with the precious blood of Christ, as of a lamb without blemish and without spot" (1 Peter 1:18-19). The Lord Jesus Christ took our sins in His body to the tree (1 Peter 2:24) and there gained for sinful man something which could never have been obtained in any other way. He reconciled sinners to God and made it possible for guilty people to be accepted into the family of God. His teaching enlightened intellects, but His death and resurrection transformed lives.

> I need no other argument; I need no other plea;
> It is enough that Jesus died, and that He died for me.

*The Lamb of sustenance (Exod. 29:26-27)*

Moses was very explicit in his instructions to Aaron. He was careful in explaining the procedure to be followed in sacrifices brought to the altar of God. Part of the animal was for Jehovah as a sacrifice, but part was given to the officiating priests. The same lamb which was slain also supplied food for the priests. The sons of Aaron needed sustenance. This seemingly insignificant detail suggests other truths of greater significance. The Savior was the Lamb of God sent from heaven. The purpose of His mission was linked with the Passover feast and the celebration of the Last Supper. Speaking of His body, His flesh, the Lord said, "He that eateth of this bread shall live forever" (John 6:58). "And he took bread and gave thanks, and brake it, and gave unto them saying, This is my body which is given for you: this do in remembrance of me" (Luke 22:19). Even in eternity, the Savior will be our source of spiritual nourishment. "For the Lamb. . .shall feed them, and shall lead them unto living fountains of waters" (Rev. 7:17).

*The Lamb of service (Ezek. 34:2)*

Wool can be obtained only from sheep, and from the commencement of human history, men learned how to take it and make garments. Frequently throughout the Old Testament, reference was made to such clothing. Leviticus 13:47 speaks of the woolen garments of a leper, and Deuteronomy 22:11 describes the inadvisability of wearing woolen and linen garments together. The chief source of raw material used in the making of woolen clothing was sheep. It is thought-provoking, therefore, that the Bible describes the garments made possible by the Lamb of God. Isaiah 61:10 speaks of the garments of salvation—a gift from the Lord. Evidently, the ancients realized that silk and linen were beautiful, but for warmth and protection in a storm, nothing equalled wool. To be clothed in the righteousness of the Lamb of God is the only protection from eternal storms.

When He shall come with trumpet sound
Oh, may I then in Him be found:
*Clothed in His righteousness alone,*
Faultless to stand before the throne.

# A TEACHER...FROM GOD

(JOHN 3:2)

This name was given to the Savior by Nicodemus, the greatest theologian in Israel. To a degree, all rabbis were teachers, but some were nomads; they wandered from town to town offering counsel and accepting food from their students and friends. Nicodemus was aware of the life-style of the Lord; how He traversed the highways and byways preaching about righteousness, and the conclusion that Jesus was a teacher was inevitable. Yet, he perceived something other observers did not see. He said, "We know that thou art a teacher *come from God;* for no man can do these miracles that thou doest, except God be with him" (John 3:2). That placed the Lord in a special category. There was no rival—no competitor—doing identical work.

*He taught by exemplary practice (Luke 11:1)*

Jesus practiced what He taught. Some teachers say, "Don't do as I do, do as I say," and often their example ruins their testimony. Unquestionably, the Savior was the greatest Teacher who ever lived, but the effectiveness of His remarks was enhanced by the glorious example given to His followers. Luke described one of these events. "And it came to pass, that, as he was praying in a certain place, when he ceased, one of his disciples said unto him, Lord, teach us to pray, even as John also taught his disciples" (Luke 11:1). To pray was a daily practice among all Jews, but as the disciples watched and listened to their Lord, they evidently became aware that His prayers were different. When Jesus prayed, something happened! When they prayed, nothing happened. Their request revealed the intense longing within their souls. What Jesus said was important, but what He did was even more vital to the effectiveness of His teaching.

*He taught through expository preaching (John 6:48-50)*

Almost everything Jesus preached was related to the Old Testament Scriptures. He quoted the writings of the prophets and explained their statements. For example, when Jesus spoke to Nicodemus, He referred to the time when Moses lifted up the serpent in the wilderness. Having drawn attention to the famous incident, the Lord explained how He would be the fulfillment of the ancient type. Jesus taught concerning the bread, or manna, which fell during the years of Israel's pilgrimage and then claimed He was the *True* Bread which had been sent from heaven. People could eat and live forever. Paul's injunction to Timothy remains one of the most important commands in the Word of God. The young minister was told to *preach the Word.* A sermon without the Bible, is only an eloquent essay. ''And Ezra the scribe stood upon a pulpit of wood, which they had made for the purpose. . . . And Ezra opened the book in the sight of all the people. . . . So they read in the book in the law of God distinctly, *and gave the sense,* and caused them to understand the reading'' (Neh. 8:4, 5, 8).

*He taught by enlightening parables (Matt. 13:3)*

Jesus was a master of the art of telling stories. He had the ability to describe common things and make them vehicles through which to impart wisdom. His parables became immortal. He spoke of the sower, the tares and the wheat, the drag-net, the mustard seed, the pearl of great price, and many other things. His stories were like windows in a house; they admitted light. Jesus spoke of lilies of the field and stated that even Solomon in all his glory was not arrayed as were they. He spoke of a small sparrow falling injured to the ground and declared that this could not happen without the Father in heaven being aware of the event. When the Lord explained that God was like the father of the prodigal son, He opened vistas of loveliness never before seen. Jesus used parables, and multitudes attended His meetings. He was different! He was marvelous, and millions of people agree with the officers who said, ''Never man spake like this man'' (John 7:46).

# THE BRIDEGROOM

(JOHN 3:29; REVELATION 21:9)

Since the dawn of history, male and female have complemented each other, and their mutual affections and desires have culminated in matrimony and parenthood. Perhaps the earliest glimmerings of this desire for fellowship may be detected in God's creation of man. Jehovah needed a special kind of friendship and planned to walk and talk with man in Eden. Union between man and woman should be the most hallowed experience in life. A wedding signifies *dignity, desire,* and *delight.* The dignity of providing, the desire to participate, and the delight each one has in pleasing the other are all part of marriage.

*The bridegroom in Jewish predictions*

The prophets had much to relate regarding the ultimate purposes of God. It was God who inaugurated, sanctioned, and blessed marriage; He performed the first wedding on the earth. Adam was made to sleep, and from his side God took that which became woman. Many years later, the last Adam was also placed in a deep sleep at Calvary, and out of that experience God took that which, under His blessing, became the Church—the Bride. The marriage of Isaac also supplied veiled foreshadowings of the plans of the Almighty. Abraham dispatched his most trusted servant to seek a bride in a foreign land. The patriarch decided it was not good for Isaac to dwell alone and therefore sent his servant with glad tidings to a maid in a distant country. When she responded to the love of one she had never seen, the groundwork was laid for the most delightful wedding ever witnessed. Similarly, God sent the Holy Spirit to seek a bride for Christ. The ancient question, "Wilt thou go with this man?" sounds familiar to every Christian.

*The bridegroom in John's preaching*

When dissension and doubt appeared among the followers of John, he said to them: "Ye yourselves bear me witness, that I said, I am not the Christ, but that I am sent before him. He that hath the bride is the bridegroom: but the friend of the bridegroom, which standeth and heareth him, rejoiceth greatly because of the bridegroom's voice: this my joy, therefore, is fulfilled. He must increase, but I must decrease" (John 3:28-30). This was the first time the Savior was given that name by a New Testament character. The Lord was to become a bridegroom and therefore would seek a bride. That the Bridegroom would enjoy the friendship of others was evident, and the wilderness preacher rejoiced in that this privilege had been given to him. He had recognized the Groom and was acquainted with His voice; they were friends! Later, it became even more significant that Jesus was seeking a bride, for in speaking of His return to earth, He spoke of ten virgins who went forth to meet the bridegroom (see Matt. 25:1-13). The gospel would be preached to all nations, and the Holy Spirit—as was the case in the wedding of Isaac—would seek a bride for the Savior.

*The bridegroom in Jehovah's presence*

John said, "And the angel talked with me, saying, Come hither, I will shew thee the bride, the Lamb's wife" (Rev. 21:9). Earlier (19:7), the cry of a great multitude said, "Let us be glad and rejoice, and give honor to him: *for the marriage of the Lamb is come,* and his wife [bride] hath made herself ready." No author, preacher, or angel is sufficiently eloquent to describe the glory of that resplendent event. We are not informed of the extent of God's celestial kingdom, but it is known that millions of angels exist to do the will of their Creator. When the marriage of the Lamb takes place, and when Christ claims His blood-washed bride, that ceremony will be the center of eternal attention. Angelic anthems will echo throughout eternity as innumerable voices sing, "Worthy is the Lamb." "Blessed are they which are called unto the marriage supper of the Lamb" (Rev. 19:9). All seats for that banquet must be reserved in advance. Latecomers will never be admitted!

# A JEW

(JOHN 4:9)

Throughout the ages, the name "Jew" has been associated with ignominy and shame; to belong to the stigmatized Hebrews was a detriment hard to overcome. Unfortunately, even some of the chosen race tried to hide their lineage because it threatened danger and death. The modern world should never forget Hitler's infamy when millions of Jews were systematically exterminated in the gas ovens of Nazi Germany. Those poor, haunted, desperate people fled before the approaching storm of racism, but many were unfortunately caught and killed. The gaunt, grim walls of the execution chambers remain as sordid testimonials to the depths of evil to which assassins can sink in their quest for domination.

When Jesus was upon the earth, the situation was not as serious. The Jews lived in their own land observing Hebrew laws. Yet, even then, Roman soldiers occupied the country and extorted taxes from people who were reluctant to pay. The Samaritans, who were half-Jews, detested their neighbors, and the dislike was mutual. Adjacent Gentile nations shared the bitterness, and although Caesar's armies maintained peace within the land, the smouldering animosity could not be hidden.

*An enlightening remark (John 4:9)*

The Samaritan woman was very surprised when she saw the Stranger sitting at Sychar's well. She was more startled when He asked for a drink of water. She said, "How is it that thou, *being a Jew,* asketh drink of me, which am a woman of Samaria? For the Jews have no dealings with the Samaritans." Her statement revealed the immense social barriers which existed between the two races. Apparently, there was neither bitterness nor animosity in her soul when she conversed with Jesus. She was greatly surprised that a Jew would fraternize with a Samaritan. She did not understand that the love of God knows no racial barriers and that His kindness extends to all people. She called Him "Jew" because she had no way of knowing He was neither Jew nor Gentile—He was the God-Man, deity manifested in human form.

*An emphatic reminder (Acts 10:28)*

When Cornelius, a centurion of the Italian band, sent for Peter, the apostle was reluctant to respond to the request of a Gentile soldier. Nevertheless, when God intervened, ordering His servant to go as requested, Peter went to the stranger's home to say, "Ye know how it is an unlawful thing for a man that is a Jew to keep company, or come unto one of another nation; but God hath shewed me that I should not call any man common or unclean" (read Acts

10:17-29). The woman at Sychar's well mentioned a regrettable characteristic of the Jews, but Simon Peter reminded Cornelius it was *unlawful* for Jews to associate with people of an alien race. The traditions of the fathers had closed the eyes of all Jews to any virtue in the lives of foreigners. When Jesus was called a *Jew,* He was being associated with bigoted, egotistical people. The Hebrews were always detested by Gentiles, and for many centuries have been the victims of persecutors. That was perhaps one of the reasons why they crucified Jesus.

*An excellent revelation (Rom. 2:28-29)*

It is thought-provoking to read the message which Paul sent to the church in Rome. The apostle was a Jew who was intensely proud of his heritage. He wrote: "For he is not a Jew who is one outwardly; neither is that circumcision, which is outward in the flesh: but he is a Jew which is one inwardly; and circumcision is that of the heart, in the spirit, and not in the letter; whose praise is not of men, but of God." When the Hebrews were first called *Jews,* it was an indication God expected them to be a separated, consecrated group of men and women as His chosen representatives on earth. Unfortunately, this early vision was lost. Jesus came to create *another race of dedicated people.* Through His redemptive work, *the true Jews* would belong to all nations. Laws would apply to the inner life and not be confined to ordinances. Holiness and consecration would be the hallmarks of God's saints. Jews and Gentiles would be unified in Christ. They would be *true Jews,* conformed to the image of God's Son (see Rom. 8:29 and 1 John 3:2).

# THE SAVIOR OF THE WORLD

(JOHN 4:42)

This was one of the most attractive names ever given to the Lord. It was warm, inviting, and self-explanatory. Throughout the history of the human race, people have always been experts at getting into trouble. Isaiah, the prophet, was not surprised when the Lord said, "Look unto me and be ye saved all the ends of the earth; for I am God, and there is none else" (Isa. 45:21-22). Jehovah was the *Savior* of His people, and it was significant that Jesus inherited that name. The angel who announced His birth said, "Fear not; for, behold, I bring you tidings of great joy, which shall be to all people. For unto you is born this day in the city of David a Savior, which is Christ the Lord" (Luke 2:10-11).

*What He became . . . a Savior for sinners . . . the great mission*

"And we have seen and do testify that the Father sent the Son to be *the Savior of the world*" (1 John 4:14). There was a glorious certainty in all the messages written by John. He had seen and thus was sure of his facts. Probably, he remembered the account included in his Gospel. The Samaritans who had listened to a sinful woman went to see and hear Jesus, and their testimony was very convincing. They said, "Now we believe, not because of thy saying; for we have heard him ourselves, and know that this is indeed the Christ, *the Savior of the world*" (John 4:42). Doubtless, this was one of the most exciting incidents in the lives of the disciples. The Samaritans were considered to be beyond the reach of God's care. They were defiled outcasts with whom no orthodox Jew associated. To these estranged people Jesus went, thus providing evidence that no man or nation is beyond the reach of God's love.

*What He remains . . . a Savior for saints . . . the great ministry*

The saving ministry of the Lord Jesus did not terminate when He died; it became greater in its dimension. His atoning death dealt with our wickedness; His ministry at God's right hand effectively deals with our weakness. What He began when He redeemed sinners by His precious blood, He will complete. "He ever liveth to make intercession for us." The writer to the Hebrews, who emphasized this fact, said, "Let us therefore come boldly unto the throne of grace, that we may obtain mercy, and find grace to help in time of need" (Heb. 4:16). The Samaritans believed Jesus was the Savior for the entire world. Paul in Galatians 6:10 mentions *the household of faith* and in Ephesians 2:19 refers to *the household of God.* Evidently, the high priestly ministry of the Savior reached all who, through faith, entered into a relationship with God. He planned that they should be conformed to His perfect image.

*What He will become . . . a Savior for suppliants . . . the great miracle*

God's love has always been greater than man's sin. Although the Jewish nation resisted His loving advances and crucified their Messiah, they remained the chosen people. The Bible states that some day these people will recognize Him to be their Savior. When oppressed by overwhelming forces and threatened with extinction, Israel will see their Messiah standing upon the Mount of Olives. "And one shall say unto him, What are these wounds in thine hands? Then he shall answer, Those with which I was wounded in the house of my friends" (Zech. 13:6). "In that day there shall be a fountain opened to the house of David and to the inhabitants of Jerusalem for sin and uncleanness" (Zech. 13:1).

Perhaps in some unrevealed fashion, the Lord will be our Savior throughout eternity. Before time commenced there was an insurrection in heaven when Lucifer, a created angel, rebelled against the authority of God. That will never happen again, for through the countless ages of eternity, the Lord will remain with His bride. His presence will be the guarantee that sin will never again darken the horizons of God's celestial country.

# THE JUDGE

(JOHN 5:22)

When John was permitted to describe the glory of the risen and exalted Lord, he used strange and exciting words, "And I turned to see the voice that spake with me. And being turned, I saw. . .one like unto the Son of man, clothed with a garment down to the foot, and girt about the paps [chest] with a golden girdle. His head and his hairs were white like wool, as white as snow" (Rev. 1:12-14). All British people are interested in the attire of American lawyers. Although judges wear black robes, the attorneys often appear without jackets and sometimes with shirt sleeves rolled up. This is not the case in a British court. There, judges and lawyers wear white, wooly wigs, and one wonders if this procedure were first inspired by John's description of the Judge among the candlesticks. Among men, the black robe reminds of the seriousness and solemnity of the occasion, and the white wigs suggest the righteousness by which the case is tried.

*The competence of the judge*

"For the Father judgeth no man, but hath committed all judgment unto the Son" (John 5:22). The laws of a nation require that judges be elected to office. The more important the assignment, the more stringent become the qualifications. A president may nominate a man to be a justice of the Supreme Court, but an enquiry into the nominee's life sometimes results in his being pronounced unfit for office. Judges are expected to be examples of the highest standard of moral law. It is significant that God chose Jesus to be the Judge of men; there was no blemish in His record. Not only was He without sin, He was also conversant with the laws of God and qualified to judge any case brought before Him. Judges sometimes ask that a case be tried in another court; they feel incompetent to pass judgment and disqualify themselves. Abraham referred to Jehovah as "the Judge of all the earth" (Gen. 18:25), but with the passing of time, God decided to ask Another to assume the responsibility of becoming the Judge of all people. The nominee was Jesus, God's Son.

*The case before the judge*

"And I saw a great white throne, and him that sat on it, from whose face the earth and the heaven fled away. . . .And I saw the dead, small and great, stand before God" (Rev. 20:11-12). The writer to the Hebrews stated, "It is appointed unto men once to die, but *after this the judgment*" (Heb. 9:27). The reliability of Christ, the Judge, was attested by His own statement: "I can of mine own self do nothing: as I hear, I judge, *and my judgment is just;* because I seek not mine own will, but the will of my Father which hath sent me'' (John 5:30). The Bible teaches that at the end of time, men will stand before God to answer for their conduct upon earth. John drew attention to ''the Lamb's book of life'' (Rev. 21:27), and indicated that only those people whose names were written in that book would be eligible to live in the heavenly Jerusalem. Jesus said to those who rejected Him, ''Ye shall die in your sins: whither I go, ye cannot come'' (John 8:21). No one could be more competent to judge sinners than He who so often begged admission to their unrepentant souls.

*The condemnation from the judge*

Witnesses are called in every court of law, for any testimony which bears on the case is considered important in assessing the guilt of the accused. Jesus indicated this would also happen at the end of time. ''The men of Nineveh shall rise in judgment with this generation, and shall condemn it: because they repented at the preaching of Jonas; and, behold, a greater than Jonas is here. The queen of the south shall rise up in the judgment with this generation, and shall condemn it: for she came from the uttermost parts of the earth to hear the wisdom of Solomon; and, behold, a greater than Solomon is here'' (Matt. 12:41-42). The Ninevites heard God's message and repented of their sins. The Queen of Sheba heard news of Solomon and could not rest until she ascertained whether or not it was true. To hear of salvation and be indifferent to its message will be sufficient to merit judgment when sinners are pronounced guilty at the bar of divine justice. Jesus said, ''He that hath an ear, let him hear what the Spirit saith unto the churches'' (Rev. 2:7).

# THE WORKER

(JOHN 5:36)

Work can be a drudgery or a delight, a cause for continuing complaining or a source of deepening pleasure. God sanctified and blessed honest labor, and a study of His successful workmen can be illuminating to all students. Men who cease to work often die prematurely. They who remain active, even in retirement, prolong their days. Wise men and women never become loungers! Christians should always be active in the service of their Lord. It is stimulating to remember that Jesus was a worker and an untiring laborer for God so that and although He died at an early age, He left a record of success which has never been equaled.

*The worker's constant desire . . . to please his master*

It must be remembered that although the Lord Jesus belonged to the Divine Family, He "made himself of no reputation, and took upon him the form of a servant, and was made in the likeness of men: And being found in fashion as a man, he humbled himself, and became obedient unto death, even the death of the cross" (Phil. 2:7-8). Jesus did not come to earth to demonstrate how God would overcome evil. He came as a man and was totally surrendered as such to the Holy Spirit, who revealed how men should—and could—live. It was in this capacity that Jesus became a workman laboring for God. The Lord said, "I do nothing of myself; but as my Father hath taught me, I speak these things. . . . I do always those things that please him" (John 8:28-29). There was never any disagreement between God and His special Workman; they shared unbroken fellowship, and either was satisfied with the other. As the divine Workman, Jesus began each day looking to "His Master" for guidance; and it is thought-provoking that prior to every major decision, He went into the mountain to pray.

*The worker's continuing duty . . . to work according to the master plan*

Prior to the commencement of any important project, it is necessary to have a master plan. Architects place on paper a sketch of what is desired, expert attention is given to every detail of the project, and when the blueprints are completed, the plans are given to the workmen. God's master plan of redemption was perfect. He obviously knew that tragedy would befall His creation and that something would need to be done to rescue man from peril. Readers of the New Testament are acquainted with what is called "God's Plan of Salvation," for the apostles described how the Savior bore our sins to the cross. That this was all clear to the Almighty—even before it happened—boggles the mind and, to a degree, defies expression. Yet, it is indisputable that when Jesus came to earth, *the blueprints of salvation* had already been completed and that the primary task of God's special Workman was to bring to fruition that which had been planned in eternity. Throughout His ministry, Jesus never deviated from that plan but did exactly what was required.

*The worker's consummate delight. . . to behold his completed task*

When an artist is pleased with his painting, he looks upon it with justifiable pride. When an engineer beholds his finished construction, words are inadequate to express his delight. When a surgeon sees a patient fully recovered after a serious operation, a sigh of satisfaction announces the pleasure occasioned by successful surgery. Language could never express the happiness known by Christ when He saw the completion of His assigned work. Before the Savior died, He exclaimed triumphantly, "It is finished" (John 19:30), and thereafter was exalted to God's right hand. "But this man, after he had offered one sacrifice of sins forever, sat down on the right hand of God; from henceforth expecting till his enemies be made his footstool" (Heb. 10:12-13). Thus did God's Master-Workman complete His task. His tremendous achievement won for Him the approbation of God, the praise of angels, and the gratitude of every redeemed man and woman.

# THE BREAD OF LIFE

(JOHN 6:35)

The sixth chapter of John's Gospel contains some of the most important statements made by the Savior. Jesus continually emphasized that He was the Bread of Life sent down from heaven and compared His coming with the manna which sustained Israel in the wilderness. Unfortunately, the people who witnessed the feeding of the thousands failed to recognize the importance of that miraculous event. They either ignored or forgot its implications, for they asked, "What sign showest thou then, that we may see, and believe thee? What dost thou work?" (John 6:30). The question revealed that they were as stupid as their ancestors. The inference derived from Christ's statement was obvious. Without the heaven-sent manna, Israel would have perished. Similarly, without Jesus, the Living Bread from heaven, sinners would die.

*Bread is universal. . . it is for everybody*

Certain expensive foods are beyond the reach of impoverished people and can only be obtained by rich citizens of earth. Other rare products are available only in privileged countries. Yet, bread is accessible to all nations. The poor need it, but even wealthy people require the nourishment it supplies. Other commodities may please the taste, but everybody needs bread. When that alone is obtainable among poor people, it is sufficient to sustain life. Perhaps the Lord had these thoughts in mind when He claimed to be the Bread of Life. He came to be within reach of all nations.

*Bread is unique. . . it must be supplied*

Fruit grows on trees, but bread has to be supplied! Unless someone grinds the corn, makes the flour, and bakes the dough, bread would never be available to hungry people. Similarly, the manna eaten by Israel had to be supplied. It was not found on trees nor plants—God had to send it (see Exod. 16:12-14). There were no stores in the wilderness, but even if there had been, no trader could have sold what he did not possess. The Lord knew this was true of Himself. The nations of the world could never supply what starving sinners required. The Living Bread from heaven had to be supplied by God Himself. Jesus said, "This is that bread which came down from heaven: not as your fathers did eat manna, and are dead: he that eateth of this bread shall live forever" (John 6:58).

*Bread is useless. . . unless eaten*

Neglected and left on a shelf, bread becomes stale and unpalatable; and when filled with mold, it rots. The children of Israel were reminded of this truth when their supplies became useless. Unless people accept what is offered and eat what has been prepared, bread cannot help them. Jesus emphasized this truth. He encouraged His listeners to accept what God supplied and assured them that if they obeyed His commands, they would "live forever." To know the value of the Bread of Life is insufficient. To admire what is proclaimed about its sustaining virtues cannot strengthen the body. It is necessary to appropriate these qualities and to absorb them into our system so that the bread can minister to the deepest physical need. These truths apply to Christ. With Him we live, without Him we die.

Paul, the famous leper in Lambaland, Central Africa, told me his favorite Bible story was the feeding of the thousands. He said, "The loaf of bread reminds me of the mercy of God. There is a piece for every person—if only he will take it!" Blessed is the man who knows where living bread can be obtained and never rests until he has it!

# THE LIGHT OF THE WORLD

(JOHN 8:12)

Holman Hunt's famous painting "The Light of the World" has caused conflicting comments throughout the church. It depicts Christ knocking on a closed door. Unfortunately, or otherwise, the Lord is seen holding a lantern! The artist's representation is indisputably superb, but many viewers have questioned the wisdom of including a lamp in the picture. Could He who claimed to be the "Light of the World" have needed light for His feet? Perhaps, if Mr. Hunt could begin again, he might omit the lamp from his design and substitute radiance emanating from the Lord.

*Light for those in darkness (Luke 18:42)*

It is interesting to remember that light always played an important part in the experiences of Israel. During their wanderings in the wilderness, a cloud hovered above the tabernacle by day, and a flame of fire burned brightly during the night. They were evidence of the abiding presence of God (Num. 9:16-17). When Gideon's army decreased to three hundred men, they were told to place lamps inside pitchers. At a given signal, the vessels were broken so that the light could shine in the night (Judg. 7:16). Light shining in the darkness was a continuing theme within the Scriptures. It was, therefore, no cause for amazement when Jesus announced He was the "Light of the World." Two types of illumination are mentioned in the Bible. First, there was the gift of sight to the blind. Blind beggars came to Christ, and their faith was rewarded when He answered their prayers and opened their eyes. Secondly, Jesus was also capable of opening the eyes of their understanding to greater revelations of God.

*Light for those in delusion (John 8:1-12)*

It is significant that the name now being considered was first announced after an adulteress was accused before the Savior. She had been taken in the act of sin, and her ruthless accusers were anxious to obtain the opinion of Jesus. Momentarily refusing to reply to their question, the Lord wrote on the ground. Finally, He said, "He that is without sin among you, let him first cast a stone at her" (John 8:7). Throughout the embarrassing ordeal, the unfortunate woman continued to stare at the Lord, and, eventually, her faith grasped something beyond the purchasing power of money. When she called Jesus "Lord," it was evident she was beginning to see! The Lord rewarded her faith by saying, "Neither do I condemn thee; go, and sin no more" (John 8:11). It was then He announced the immortal words, "I am the light of the world; he [or she] that followeth me shall not walk in darkness, but shall have the light of life.'' Transformation of character is a far greater miracle than the opening of the eyes of a blind beggar. Some people with excellent eyesight have no vision. Others with no eyesight can look into another world.

*Light for those in danger (2 Cor. 3:15-16)*

Referring to the Jews the apostle said, ''But even unto this day, when Moses is read, the vail is upon their heart. Nevertheless, when it shall turn to the Lord, the vail shall be taken away.'' He also wrote, ''I have great heaviness and continual sorrow in my heart. For I could wish that myself were accursed from Christ for my brethren, my kinsmen according to the flesh'' (Rom. 9:2-3). Although Paul was commissioned to be the apostle to the Gentiles, he could not forget the plight of his Jewish brethren. Throughout his ministry he preached in synagogues, and more often than not, his actions led to suffering. He tried to be a light shining in their darkness, but, unfortunately, they had no desire to see. When drapes cover a window, sunlight cannot enter a room. When prejudice warps the mind, even Christ remains helpless.

# THE DOOR

(John 10:9)

Doors are among the most common things in the world. There are ornate doors of cathedrals, steel doors to vaults in a bank, canvas doors to tents, large and small doors in all kinds of vehicles, glass doors to greenhouses, and every other kind imaginable in homes throughout the world. They can be expensive or inexpensive, strong or weak, beautiful or unattractive, but they have one thing in common—they are doors! When the Savior claimed to be *the door of the sheepfold,* He enunciated truths which demand consideration. Actually, most of the sheepfolds to be found in Middle East countries have no door; they have a doorway—the shepherd becomes the door, and entrance is only possible when he permits it.

*A door is a means of entrance*

A building without a door is a vault, sealed in death. A divine plan without a door would be meaningless, unreachable, useless. Christ came to be the means whereby those who were afar off might come near. There was but one door in Noah's ark; there was only one door in the tabernacle in the wilderness. "Neither is there salvation in any other; for there is none other name under heaven given among men; whereby we must be saved" (Acts 4:12). There is but *one* Door. Jesus said, "I am the way, the truth, and the life: no man cometh unto the Father, but by me" (John 14:6). There are many religions and many sects, but there is only *one* Savior. God has revealed clearly that Christ is the only highway to eternal blessedness. Men who ignore His words exhibit stupidity.

*A door is a means of separation*

To be on the one side of a closed door means to be separated, or cut off, from those on the other side. Seldom is a door used as an ornament! Doors are made to be used, and when this is done, a person passes from one place to another. There is a vast difference between being inside and outside; when the door is closed, it is not possible to be on both sides at once. It is thus with Christians. To respond to the claims of Christ means to forsake the company of those outside, to turn one's back upon that which is evil, and with calm deliberation to identify oneself with the people of God. When Jesus claimed to be *the Door* of the sheepfold, He implied that He would be the great divider of men. People would be either for or against Him. He would even turn parents against their children! (see Matt. 10:35-37).

*A door is a means of protection*

When the icy blasts of a midwinter storm beat upon a home, a closed door becomes a shelter. Behind its solid strength is warmth, comfort, and protection. When wild beasts or evil men enter a home, a strong door becomes a bulwark. The claim of Christ to be *the Door* suggests not only that He was inviting sinners to seek refuge in His kingdom, but also that He was promising to safeguard them in every time of stress and danger. "I will never leave thee" seems to be the talk of a truly good Shepherd. David often proved the reliability of such a promise. He wrote, "For thou hast been a shelter for me, and a strong tower from the enemy. I will abide in thy tabernacle forever: I will trust in the covert of thy wings" (Ps. 61:3-4).

*A door is a means of exclusion*

"An open door issues an invitation, a strong door promises protection, but a locked door is something to be feared. Matthew 25:10-12 suggests that all men should strive to enter the kingdom of God while the door is open. The time must come when it will close. 'Afterward came all the other virgins, saying, Lord, Lord, open to us. But he answered and said, Verily I say unto you, I know you not.'" (Quoted from the author's commentary, *John's Wonderful Gospel*, p. 214.) The Lord also said, "Strive to enter at the strait gate; for many, I say unto you, will seek to enter in, and shall not be able" (Luke 13:24). It is a serious and solemn thought that He who died to redeem sinners, will refuse some day to accept people who refused to enter His kingdom. That He will one day judge the world in righteousness should encourage all people to heed the warning message of the gospel. Doors may close in a moment and they jam sometimes, so that entrance becomes an impossibility. To be on the right side of *heaven's Door* should be the greatest ambition in a person's life.

> One door, and only one, and yet its sides are two.
> I'm on the inside, on which side are you?

# THE GOOD SHEPHERD

(John 10:11)

The children of Israel were always lovers of sheep and, therefore, from the beginning of their history, shepherds were known among the tribes. David was a shepherd boy, and much later in time, God called Amos, who also was a shepherd (Amos 7:15). Today in the western world, sheep are placed in fields and allowed to graze; only in Bible lands and a few other isolated localities are shepherds found among their flocks. It is a common sight among Bedouin tribes to see young men and boys wandering through arid country searching for pasture. I remember visiting an encampment only to discover that the men were in the desert with their sheep and camels. Later that evening, I returned to receive a great welcome from the shepherds, who had returned with their animals. That incident was my first real contact with those remarkable people of the desert.

*The Good Shepherd (John 10:11)*

Not all shepherds were *good* shepherds. A man whose thoughts were constantly in the cities and who loved noisy society hardly found pleasure in lonely places where sheep were his only companions. Throughout the ministry of Jesus, He constantly referred to His followers as sheep, and frequently affirmed that His audiences were as sheep without a shepherd (Mark 6:34). There were certain unmistakable characteristics of all good shepherds. They loved their sheep, enjoyed their company, and were willing to sacrifice much to protect them from enemies. David, the shepherd boy, killed wild animals in order to defend his flock (1 Sam. 17:34-36). The shepherd led his sheep to green pasture and thus provided their food. Without his aid, the sheep would die; without their company, the shepherd's life would be exceedingly lonely. Jesus was mindful of all these details when He said, "I am the good shepherd."

*The Great Shepherd (Heb. 13:20)*

When the writer to the Hebrews expressed his desire for the prosperity of his readers, he said, "Now the God of peace, that brought again from the dead our Lord Jesus, *that great shepherd of the sheep,*...make you perfect in every good work." It must be readily admitted that the Lord Jesus Christ was perfect in everything He did; it would have been impossible to improve upon His actions. Nevertheless, the deepening experiences of those who trusted Him inevitably led them to higher plains of understanding. The more Christ was seen and considered, the more wonderful He appeared to become. Probably, this explains why the New Testament writer tried to improve on Christ's claim to be the good Shepherd. Not all *good* shepherds are *great* ones. A man may be a *good* musician but not necessarily a *great* one. This line of demarcation may be applied in all professions. Jesus was supremely excellent in every detail of what He was and did. He loved His sheep enough to die for them. To safeguard His followers He arose from the dead, so that His constant care would always be assured. He sent His Spirit to lead and guide them into green pastures and beside still waters; their food supplies would never be in jeopardy.

*The Chief Shepherd (1 Peter 5:4)*

Simon Peter was a good student of His Lord. He never forgot the Savior's words concerning the sheep! Many years after Christ returned to heaven, Peter wrote to the pastors of the churches to say: "Feed the flock of God which is among you. . . . And when the *chief Shepherd* shall appear, ye shall receive a crown of glory that fadeth not away" (1 Peter 5:2, 4). Shepherd boys were never sent to school to be taught their trade; they learned it in the fields where they spent most of their time. Nevertheless, when we consider these three statements, we are reminded of a school. Peter suggested that all pastors should emulate the example of the Chief Shepherd, whose instructions they valued. Jesus has now become the Owner of the flock. Pastors who are under-shepherds may be assured of a glittering reward for faithful service. Perhaps this is one of the most attractive titles ever given to the Savior.

# THE MASTER

(JOHN 11:28)

The famous British theological scholar, W. E. Vine, states that there are at least seven Greek words which are translated "Master." Five of them are: (1) *didaskalos,* which means "a teacher" (Matt. 8:19); (2) *kurios,*one who exercises power (Mark 13:35); (3) *despotees*—from which comes the word "despot"—meaning absolute ownership and uncontrolled power (1 Tim. 6:1); (4) *rabbei,* an Arabic word expressing respectful address (Matt. 26:25); and (5) *epistatees*—which indicates a position of importance, especially within military circles—a chief, a commander, an overseer (Luke 5:5). This word occurs only in Luke's Gospel (8:24; 45; 9:33, 49; 17:13). The other two words are (6) *katheegeetees,* denoting a guide into truth—a teacher (Matt. 23:10) and (7) *kuberneetees*, referring to the master of a ship, a guide into strange waters or steering, a pilotage (Acts 27:11) (see Vine's *Expository Dictionary of Old and New Testament Words*, vol. 3, pp. 46-47). This enlightening commentary from such an eminent author explains how the term "Master" covers a wide area of thought and suggests a variety of interpretations.

*The Master who owns us . . . kurios* (Matt. 6:24; Mark 13:35)

The Greek word used in Matthew denotes ownership. Jesus said, "No man can serve two masters: for either he will hate the one, and love the other; or else he will hold to the one, and despise the other. Ye cannot serve God and mammon." Purchased slaves became the property of the buyer. Thereafter, the servant existed to please his lord. No one could work for another master without the permission of the legal owner. When the Lord instructed His disciples concerning the time and method of His return to this world, He said, "Watch ye therefore: for ye know not when the *master* of the house cometh." Paul expressed a similar thought when writing to the Corinthians. "For ye are bought with a price" (see 1 Cor. 6:20). The Master purchased us with His blood; therefore, we should be His faithful servants.

*The Master who instructs us . . . didaskalos* (John 20:15-17)

When Mary came to the tomb on Easter morning, she saw the risen Lord, but, "She, supposing him to be the gardener, saith unto him, Sir, if thou have borne him hence, tell me where thou hast laid him, and I will take him away. Jesus saith unto her, Mary. She turned herself, and saith unto him, Rabboni, which is to say, *Master*" (vv. 15-16). It was in that moment of revelation that the emotions imprisoned within her soul found expression. She could not understand the mysteries of His death, but Jesus was at least alive again; nothing else mattered. She cried, ''Rabboni'' (Teacher), but as she fell to embrace His feet, He stepped away from her arms and said, ''Touch me not; for I am not yet ascended to my Father; but go to my brethren, and say unto them, I ascend unto my Father, and your Father, and to my God, and your God'' (vv. 16-17). Hitherto, the title ''God'' took precedence over all other names. Henceforth, Jehovah was to be seen not primarily as God, but as *Father*. The reconciling value of Christ's death had made possible a new relationship between God and any sinner.

*The Master who leads us . . . katheegeetees* (Matt. 23:8)

When Christ condemned the daily practices of the Pharisees, He said, ''[They] love the uppermost rooms at feasts, and the chief seats in the synagogues, and greetings in the markets, and to be called of men, Rabbi, Rabbi. But be not ye called Rabbi: for one is your *Master,* even Christ; and all ye are brethren'' (Matt. 23:6-8). Contrasting Himself with the religious leaders of His time, Jesus emphasized that the disciples should follow one leader, one guide. He implied that they were sheep needing a shepherd. False leaders could not be trusted; He, the Good Shepherd, would take them to green pastures and beside still waters. His unfailing presence would be their safeguard against danger; His wisdom would be their guarantee of sustenance. The name *Master* appeared to be inclusive of everything they required. With Him they began their journey to heaven; He would be there at its end.

# THE TRUTH

(JOHN 14:6)

The glorious name *Truth* was given to Christ by Himself and represented one of the most important claims ever made! Throughout the history of Israel, many prophets claimed to have a monopoly on the truth. True messengers of Jehovah needed no vindication; what they predicted came to pass. False prophets, some of whom were sorcerers, often spoke ambiguously so that their authority could not be challenged. Although they claimed to be servants of God, they were charlatans, who made speeches to please wealthy sponsors. During that period, innumerable lies were told, and the misrepresentation of facts was commonplace. Truth was a jewel hard to find. When Jesus announced that He was the embodiment of it, His claim was sensational to say the least.

*His message was endorsed (Matt. 17:5)*

A communist once said that, with certain reservations, he could be a follower of Jesus. He said the Carpenter was the outstanding revolutionary of all time. Jesus opposed the capitalistic classes of His generation and advocated policies completely opposed to the bigots who ruled Palestine. There was an element of truth in his statement. Jesus introduced teaching which was unacceptable to the Pharisees, and conformity to His message was anathema to the priests. It is important to remember that the doctrine of the Lord was endorsed by God, and that fact should be sufficient to encourage consideration of everything Jesus uttered. When the disciples looked at the transfigured Lord on the mountain, they heard God saying, "This is my beloved Son, in whom I am well pleased; *hear ye him*" (Matt. 17:5).

*His message was emphatic*

Jesus never faltered in presenting His message. Other speakers were indecisive, but all who listened to Christ understood His remarks. He knew what needed to be said and said it! For example, He told the Pharisees, " . . . if ye believe not that I am he, ye shall die in your sins" (John 8:24). Christ was *profound* in doctrine, *pertinent* in illustrations, *practical* in applications, and *persistent* in His endeavors.

*His message has endured*

History speaks of emperors who conquered the world, but time destroyed their kingdoms. Illustrious philosophers influenced vast multitudes with their oratory, but they died and their teachings perished. Certain politicians exercised what appeared to be unlimited power over nations, but they were either deposed or succeeded by others. Nevertheless, although two thousand years have elapsed since Jesus was crucified, His authority has never been destroyed nor His teaching forgotten. He who never possessed a home now reigns in millions of dwellings in many nations. Jesus never wrote a book, but the libraries of great universities are filled with innumerable volumes written about Him. He was crucified as a malefactor; yet today kings and queens, rich and poor, educated and illiterate worship at His feet. The Savior said, "Heaven and earth shall pass away, but my words shall not pass away" (Matt. 24:35).

*His message still emancipates*

Jesus said, "Verily, verily, I say unto you, he that believeth on me, the works that I do shall he do also; *and greater works than these shall he do;* because I go unto my Father" (John 14:12). Christ never took His message beyond the borders of Palestine. The Church has preached it throughout the world. His ministry of healing was wonderful and inspiring, but, alas, it was limited to people who were near to Him. Christian doctors have erected hospitals, and millions of people are being healed in body and soul as they listen to the message taught by missionaries. When a drunken father becomes a new daddy, when a home is changed by the power of the gospel, when a despairing soul finds new life and hope for the future, that, and that alone, is irrefutable proof that the gospel of Christ—*the Truth*—continues to be "the power of God unto salvation" (Rom. 1:16).

# THE TRUE VINE

(JOHN 15:1)

The words of Jesus, "I am the true vine," might have been suggested either by the light of the moon falling on the great golden vine with which Herod had beautified the temple or by the vineyards alongside of which, or through which, the disciples walked. The moonlight possibly shone upon the spreading vine, the branches were laden with luscious fruit, and leaves gently sighed as the winds of evening moved them to and fro. The solitude was rich with the benediction of heaven, the night sky was studded with starry jewels, and the disciples were silent and apprehensive when Jesus said, "I am the true vine and my Father is the husbandman." There had been, and doubtless would be others who would claim this distinction, but He was the *true* vine. God had waited a long time to see the fruit of His planning. His expectation had been fully realized, for the Vine had responded. As the earthly husbandman would be delighted with a vine heavily laden with top quality fruit, so the Father was pleased with the Son. Christ "did always those things which pleased God" (see John 8:29). How then could the Father be anything else but extremely satisfied with the life and work of Him Whom He had sent into the world? (Quoted in part from the author's commentary, *John's Wonderful Gospel,* pp. 315-316.)

*A great example*

Possibly one of the best ways to understand the text is to compare it with Christ's other name—*the Branch* (Zech. 6:12). What Christ is to His Father, Christians should be to the Savior. The Lord Jesus gave us an example which He desires us to emulate. He abides in the center of the divine will; His followers should likewise abide in Him as He abides in God. Wise husbandmen carefully attended to the needs of the vine, and at all times the plant responded to the owner's will. That kind of relationship exists between God and His Son. There was nothing which grieved the Father, nor interfered with the fruitfulness of the Son. With calm deliberation, the Lord looked at the disciples and seemed to say, "Ye are the branches; I expect you to live as I live, to do what I command, and to follow closely the pattern now set before you."

*A gracious expectancy*

Unless a branch is supported by the tree, it falls to the ground. Its strength is continually drawn from the tree itself so that only as that union is maintained can the sap flow into the branch. If anything blocks the life-giving channel, the branch becomes a leafless skeleton silhouetted against the sky. Therefore, Jesus said, "Abide in me, and I in you. As the branch cannot bare fruit of itself, except it abide in the vine; no more can ye, except ye abide in me'' (John 15:4). Unless branches are securely joined to the tree, strong winds might rend them apart. No branch can exist without the supportive power of the tree. To maintain such strength, it becomes increasingly necessary that this union be strengthened. Christ and His followers belong to each other; nothing should destroy that fellowship.

*A glorious exuberancy*

The entire purpose of a vine is fruitbearing. John mentioned fruit (15:2), more fruit (15:2), and much fruit (15:5 and 8) and then described how Jesus said, ''These things have I spoken unto you, that my joy might remain in you, and that your joy might be full'' (15:11). An unproductive branch could never please the parent tree. Likewise, a disappointing Christian cannot be a source of joy for his Lord. It is not known whether trees, vines, and other plants can communicate, but if they do, it should be easy to recognize displeasure when withered branches ruin an expected harvest. Perhaps this was one reason why Paul urged his readers not to grieve the Holy Spirit (see Eph. 4:30). There is probably no other name which reveals the intimate relationship between Christ and His followers as does this title—*the Vine.* His joy is dependent upon our fruitfulness; our spiritual health is dependent upon the union preserved with the Lord. In order to achieve our greatest goals, we need each other! The Father never needed to prune His Vine, for Christ ''lived, moved, and had his being'' in the center of divine approbation. Unfortunately, we have not yet reached those exalted standards of excellence. If our Husbandman should find it necessary to use His knife, it would be wise to remember the hand which does the pruning is called *love.*

Search me, O God, and know my heart today;
Try me, O Savior, know my thoughts, I pray.
See if there be some wicked way in me:
Cleanse me from every sin and set me free.

# THE MAN

(JOHN 19:5)

This is the simplest, the most easily understood of all the names given to Christ. Yet, when it is carefully considered and traced through the New Testament, it glows with an unmistakable luster. Jesus was certainly *a man* from Nazareth, but throughout the centuries, people of all nations have exclaimed, "What a Man!" When Paul wrote to Timothy, he described the Lord as holding the most important office in the universe. "For there is one God, and one mediator between God and man, *the Man*, Christ Jesus" (1 Tim. 2:5). Writing to the Romans, the apostle stated, "For if through the offence of one many be dead, much more the grace of God, and the gift by grace, which is by one man, Jesus Christ, hath abounded unto many" (Rom. 5:15). The Mediator became humanity's link with God; the Savior became God's link with humanity. Probably the most thought-provoking statement came from Pontius Pilate. When the governor introduced his Prisoner to the clamoring crowd, he said, *"Behold the man"* (John 19:5). Later, when he addressed the people, he said, *"Behold your king"* (John 19:14). It was to be regretted that he never understood the testimony of John the Baptist, who said, "*Behold the Lamb of God* which taketh away the sin of the world" (John 1:29). Probably Pilate would never have understood how *one man* could be a sin-bearer, a royal mediator, and an eternal monarch. True faith easily discerns these facts, but Pilate, whose vision was impaired by unbelief, could only say, *"Behold the Man."*

*Subjected to temptation . . . He resisted (Heb. 4:15)*

It has always been difficult to fathom the uncharted depths of the statement in the letter to the Hebrews. "Jesus the Son of God . . . was *in all points* tempted like as we are, yet without sin" (Heb. 4:14-15). Throughout the history of the Church, theologians have argued regarding the possibilities associated with the temptations of the Savior. Some have asserted that His divinity made it impossible for Christ to sin (compare Heb. 6:18). Others have claimed that Jesus could not have been tempted *in all points* as we are because He did not have an evil nature inherited from His parents. All humans can repeat the words of David: "Behold, I was shapen in iniquity; and in sin did my mother conceive me" (Ps. 51:5). This was not true in connection with the birth of the Lord. He was sinless. It has been asked, "How then could He know the problems of lust, covetousness, and the other ramifications of human desire?" The answer to these questions may be beyond our comprehension, but we may be sure that when Satan attempted to overcome the Savior, he used every means possible. During those frightening moments of intimidation and danger, Jesus remembered the Word of God and used it to offset the attacks of the evil one. The Lord was intensely human.

*Surrounded by trouble . . . He responded (John 6:5-6)*

David said, "Thou . . . art acquainted with all my ways" (Ps. 139:3), and this could be repeated by every Christian. The Lord knew about every circumstance which beset His followers. He belonged to a family where problems were often overwhelming; He lived with others where strife was not unknown. Throughout His ministry He met people for whom life had become a nightmare but always responded to their needs. His assistance was of incalculable worth. The Lord proved Himself to be the best of men, and no stranger was ever beyond the reach of His outstretched hand.

*Seeing their triumph . . . He rejoiced (Luke 10:21)*

"In that hour Jesus rejoiced in spirit, and said, I thank thee, O Father." When the disciples told the Lord of their triumphs, He shared their happiness. The writer to the Hebrews wrote about the Savior, "who for the joy that was set before him, endured the cross, despising the shame, and is set down at the right hand of the throne of God" (Heb. 12:2). Jesus knew what it was to hunger and to thirst as well as to be frustrated, tired, lonely, and annoyed. Often He was disappointed and exceedingly sad. At varying times He wept, and yet at other times His joy was intense. He experienced the exhilaration of the mountaintop but was aware of problems in the valley. He attracted wise men from distant lands, touched lepers in His own country, and proved that He was *"acquainted with all our ways."* It seems incomprehensible that God's Son, by whose word everything came into being, should be interested in the problems of His unworthy servants. He was never a *distant* Jehovah. He lived, moved, and had His being among men whom He loved. With believers of all nations, we also can exclaim, "What a Man!"

# THE LORD JESUS CHRIST

(ACTS 2:36; ROMANS 13:14)

Sir Robert Anderson, a true representative of British dignity and tradition, was always displeased when thoughtless Christians failed to give to Christ His proper title. Commoners always address the king or queen as "Your Majesty." Sir Robert affirmed that similar recognition should be given to the King of heaven. His full title should be *Lord Jesus Christ.* Peter would agree with this statement, for he said, "Therefore let all the house of Israel know assuredly, that God hath made that same Jesus, whom ye have crucified, both Lord and Christ" (Acts 2:36). This was probably the most comprehensive of all the names given to the Savior, for it embraced His past, present, and future. He was Lord from all eternity, He became Jesus of Nazareth, and the Bible predicts that at the end of time He will be recognized as the true Messiah who will deliver Israel.

*The Supreme Sovereign . . . what He was*

Probably the clearest definition was given by Paul when he charged Timothy "that thou keep this commandment without spot, unrebukable, until the appearing of our Lord Jesus Christ: which in his times he shall shew, who is the blessed and only Potentate, the King of kings, and Lord of lords; who only hath immortality, dwelling in the light which no man can approach unto; whom no man hath seen, nor can see: to whom be honor and power everlasting. Amen" (1 Tim. 6:14-16). Only on very infrequent occasions was man permitted to gaze into the eternal habitation of the Most High, but what he saw left him speechless with amazement. Heaven is a place where perfection is ordinary, where superlatives are incapable of expressing the surpassing excellence of all that exists in the presence of Almighty God. Little is known of the grandeur and extent of God's universal kingdom; the number of angels has never been determined. Yet, at the center of the everlasting splendor stands Christ, and before Him bows the entire population of that eternal kingdom. He is the Lord of Creation.

*The suggested subservience . . . what He became*

Writing to the Philippians, Paul said, "Let this mind be in you which was also in Christ Jesus: who being in the form of God, thought it not robbery to be equal with God; but made himself of no reputation, and took upon him the form of a servant, and was made in the likeness of men: and being found in fashion as a man, he humbled himself, and became obedient unto death, *even the death of the cross.* Wherefore God also hath highly exalted him, and given him a name which is above every name . . ." (Phil. 2:5-9). It is almost beyond comprehension that He who fills eternity with His glory should become man. He was called Jesus to indicate that the Almighty God had descended to earth to become a Savior. He voluntarily put aside the robes of His majesty and became subject to human limitations. Fully identified with humans, Jesus was able to share their problems and understand their difficulties. Thousands of His compatriots looked into His eyes, but only a few realized they were gazing into the face of God.

*The scintillating splendor . . . what He will become*

The Greek word *Christos* is the translation of the Hebrew word which meant "the Anointed One." It is frequently used in the New Testament to indicate the Messiah. When the woman at Sychar's well spoke of the expected Deliverer, Jesus replied, "I that speak unto thee am he" (see John 4:25-26). Unfortunately, Jesus "came unto his own, and his own received him not" (John 1:11). The Messiah became "the despised and rejected of men; a man of sorrows and acquainted with grief" (Isa. 53:3). Nevertheless, His rejection at that time did not change the fact that God promised to honor His Son. Jesus will yet become the accepted Messiah of the Jewish nation, and will save them from destruction. Speaking through the prophet Zechariah, God said, "And I will pour upon the house of David, and upon the inhabitants of Jerusalem, the spirit of grace and of supplication, and they shall look upon him whom they have pierced" (Zech. 12:10). "In that day there shall be a fountain opened to the house of David and to the inhabitants of Jerusalem for sin and for uncleanness" (Zech. 13:1). "And the LORD shall be king over all the earth. In that day there shall be one LORD, and his name one" (Zech. 14:9).

Yesterday, today, forever,
Jesus is the same:
All may change, but Jesus never,
Glory to His Name.

# THE PRINCE OF LIFE

(ACTS 3:15)

"The Prince of Life" was a remarkable name because it could only have been given by the Holy Spirit. Simon Peter was the speaker by whom it was mentioned, but only a few weeks earlier he had denied his Lord. The death of the Savior challenged his faith, and even after the resurrection of Jesus, Peter's disturbed emotions were expressed in his statement, "I go a fishing" (John 21:3). The apostle learned much in a short time, but, indisputably, his Teacher was the Holy Spirit. The Greek word translated "prince" was *archeegon,* which could be translated "author, giver of life," or a "predecessor in any matter" (Thayer). John wrote, "Without him was not anything made that was made" (John 1:3). Speaking to the philosophers on Mars Hill in Athens, Paul said, "He giveth to all life, and breath, and all things" (Acts 17:25). The Bible speaks of varying kinds of life. There is vegetable, animal, human, angelic, and eternal life. The Author, the Prince, the Progenitor of all these was Jesus, with whom the disciples lived. The uneducated fisherman from Galilee became a skilled expositor of truth and graduated with honor from God's university!

*How admirable . . . the Prince of Life*

The temple precincts were crowded with excited people; the dignity of the sanctuary had been completely shattered. Men and women were running all over the place and, evidently, something extraordinary had taken place. "And as the lame man which was healed held Peter and John, all the people ran together unto them in the porch that is called Solomon's, greatly wondering" (Acts 3:11). When Simon Peter saw what was happening, he began to speak to the crowd, and what followed beggared description. It is easy to analyze the apostle's speech, but it would be illuminating to read his mind. He referred to Jesus as the *Author* of life, but perhaps the translators were justified in saying, "the *Prince* of life." A prince is an uncrowned member of a royal family. He is closest to the reigning monarch and the successor to the kingdom. The listeners to the sermon in Solomon's porch remembered the Man who had recently traversed their country. Peter envisaged One who had existed before time began.

*How amazing . . . "Ye . . . killed the prince of life"*

The Son of God had given life to all things; it would appear impossible that mortal man could kill Him. If He were able to impart life to every living being, could He not prevent the destruction of His own life? There had to be some explanation for this phenomenal event. Peter was satisfied he knew the reason for the death of his Lord. Voluntarily, Christ had vacated His place in the eternal kingdom and had come to earth on a special mission. He was apparently overcome by His enemies, but the apostle knew this was only because for Him to die was part of the God-appointed mission. As Caiaphas said, "It was expedient that one man should die for the people" (John 18:14).

*How appalling . . . "But ye . . . desired a murderer to be granted unto you"*

Peter's method of contrasting Barabbas with the Lord is interesting. The Jews had chosen one who destroyed life and rejected the One who supplied it. They crucified the Healer who abolished pain and desired a robber whose exploits filled the land with violence. Their action was inexcusable and senseless. They exchanged a Prince for a slave, liberty for bondage, and a peace beyond understanding for recurring fears of insurrection. Their guilt before God was indisputable; they deserved death.

*How assured . . . "God hath raised him from the dead"*

Peter emphasized that the glorious news of the resurrection was not the product of an overwrought imagination; neither was it based on rumor. He and others had witnessed the phenomenon. His words *"whereof we are witnesses,"* challenged every doubter. He had seen the Lord and had heard His voice; his Master was alive. How could the Giver of life remain dead? Then Peter expounded the truth of *salvation through faith in Christ.* The transformed beggar presented irrefutable evidence. A dead Christ could do nothing! Yet, if Jesus were what had been claimed, there was no problem in explaining what happened to the beggar. If Christ gave life to every creature in the world, it could not have been difficult to supply strength to the cripple who sat at the gate of the temple. Simon Peter believed that His Lord had always been, and would continue to be, God's gift to dying men—the *Prince of Life.*

# THE JUSTIFIER

(ROMANS 3:26)

To be justified is to be without blame or as someone has said, "to be *just-if-I'd* never sinned." Since all people are guilty before God (Rom. 3:23), justification seemed beyond the reach of mortal beings. Debating this fact with Job, his friend Bildad the Shuhite said, "How then can a man be justified with God? Or how can he be clean that is born of a woman? Behold even to the moon . . . and the stars are not pure in his sight. How much less man, that is a worm; and the son of man, which is a worm?" (Job 25:4-6). The Pharisees realized the gravity of this disturbing situation and urged listeners to become worthy in God's sight. They believed that observance of the laws of Moses would earn favor in the sight of the Almighty. Their hopes for obtaining salvation depended upon human effort, without which sinners would perish.

*Justification denied (Ps. 143:2)*

David said, "For in thy sight, shall no man living be justified." Evidently, the psalmist realized his inability to be blameless and with an ever-increasing awareness of guilt, despaired of being free from blame. Most of his subjects shared that conviction and tried to find comfort in observing religious laws. Unfortunately, they discovered little, if any, relief in that procedure. Men were unable to keep all the laws enunciated by Moses. The harder they tried, the more they failed, for when they broke one commandment, they broke all of them.

*Justification desired (Job 25:4-6)*

The statement made by Job's friend seemed to indicate the desire within his heart. He appeared to be reaching for the unreachable. He appreciated the beauty of the stars but knew they were beyond his grasp! Others shared that conviction and in a vain search for inner peace, became hermits; pilgrims to shrines, and slaves to ordinances. The Pharisees urged people to fast, to tithe, and to perform innumerable actions in the hope of atoning for at least some of their transgressions. When Paul said, "A man is not justified by the works of the law," his statement irritated every Jewish teacher. The apostle was undermining the foundations of Hebrew theology.

*Justification declared (Rom. 3:24-26)*

Paul's teaching was diametrically opposed to every doctrine of the rabbis. He taught that what a lifetime of self-effort could not obtain, might be received in a moment. He preached that salvation depended upon what Christ had already done and not upon what man was expected to do. Jesus—the *Justifier*—was the only One capable of leading souls into a place of acceptance before God. The apostle wrote, "Being justified freely by his grace through the redemption that is in Christ Jesus: whom God hath set forth to be . . . the justifier of him which believeth in Jesus" (Rom. 3:24-26). Then, to support his assertions, Paul referred to Abraham, who was justified long before the law was given. Moses became *the leader* of Israel; Abraham had been *the father* of the nation. Paul wrote, "For if Abraham were justified by works, he hath whereof to glory; but not before God . . . Abraham believed God, *and it was counted unto him for righteousness"* (Rom. 4:1-5). Paul taught that Jesus, the Lamb of God, had taken our sins to the Cross and risen again to become the High Priest of His people. He, and He alone, could justify believers and elevate them to a state of blamelessness before the Almighty. His blood removed sins; His intercessory work pled their cause at the bar of divine Justice; His Spirit indwelt and led believers on their journey to their eternal home. Blessings thought to be beyond the reach of sinners were now obtainable. By simple faith in the Son of God, men could enter into a new relationship. Doubt and fear could be removed, for in Christ all men would be free. Paul's message was destined to live eternally. He said, "Be it known unto you therefore, men and brethren, that through this man is preached unto you the forgiveness of sins: and by him, all that believe are justified from all things, from which ye could not be justified by the law of Moses" (Acts 13:38-39).

# THE POWER AND WISDOM OF GOD

(1 Corinthians 1:24)

The names given to the Savior were always significant; they shone as jewels against the darkness of man's sin. They were facets of a diamond, each exquisitively beautiful in its own setting. Sometimes, the writers of the New Testament placed two names together, believing each one complemented the other. Paul did this when he wrote, "But unto them which are called, both Jews and Greeks, Christ *the power of God,* and *the wisdom of God.*"

*The power and wisdom of God in creation*

God's power suggests His ability to create and sustain. His wisdom provides beauty of expression and design. This becomes apparent when the somber skies of winter matches the brown and green of the trees and when in the spring of the year, sunshine and blue skies harmonize with the flowers. Who but God could create a chameleon with its inherent power of disguise? Who but a wise and thoughtful God could create camels with their built-in water pouches to make long desert journeys possible. The song of a lark on a spring morning indicates that God appreciates music. The entrancing loveliness of wild flowers suggests that the Lord specializes in color and wisdom, for then the bees make honey. People may make firecrackers, but only God can make a rainbow. Sculptors may produce clay and stone replicas of the human body, but only God breathes life. Our wonderful world reflects the eternal glories of Christ, by whose power all things came into existence. "All things were made by him, and without him, was not anything made that was made" (John 1:3).

*The power and wisdom of God in Christ*

Millions of people see the power of Christ in the stilling of the storm and the feeding of a hungry multitude. They recognize the wisdom of the Almighty in that He devised ways to redeem sinners. These facts are indisputably true, but there are other sources of information. When a woman was accused of being an adulteress, Christ displayed wisdom in the way in which He silenced the critics and power in the method by which He gave an incentive to the woman to live a cleaner life. When the Pharisees inquired about the legality of paying taxes to Caesar, Jesus asked for a coin and proceeded to preach a short but eloquent sermon from its inscription. When the authorities asked about the Lord's paying taxes, Jesus sent Peter on a fishing expedition and promised that the required money would be in the mouth of the first fish caught. His power to read the future was obvious, but His wisdom was apparent when He promised there would be sufficient money to pay for Peter and Himself (Matt. 17:27).

*The power and wisdom of God in the Church*

Writing about the unsearchable riches of Christ, Paul said, "To the intent that now unto the principalities and powers in heavenly places might be known by the church *the manifold wisdom of God,* according to the eternal purpose which he purposed in Christ Jesus our Lord" (Eph. 3:10-11). (1) *Amazing in its constitution.* Throughout the Old Testament, the human race was divided by customs and racial prejudice; people learned to despise and hate each other. Jews had no dealings with Samaritans, and all attempts to unify these people failed. That God should devise a plan by which all men could become brothers and all women sisters defied imagination. Only the wisdom of God could do this. (2) *Awesome in its capabilities.* The Church would accomplish what vast armies could not. The power of affection would supersede armaments. Without money and natural resources, missionaries would penetrate forests, cross deserts, scale mountains, and reach every part of the world. Their message would be their invincible weapon. (3) *Aware of its commitment.* The members of the Church would be impelled by supernatural energy. If it were necessary, they would be willing to endure hardship rather than attempt nothing! If one missionary died, five others would take his place; if they failed, ten more would volunteer to continue the task. There is reason to believe that the creation of the Church was the greatest miracle ever performed by God.

# OUR PASSOVER

(1 CORINTHIANS 5:7)

The Lord Jesus Christ was given many names, but none was more important than this one. The Passover feast was the most beloved institution in Israel; it reminded the nation of the deliverance of their ancestors from bondage in Egypt. If Paul's sermons in the synagogues resembled the message expressed in the letter to the Corinthian church, it would explain why almost every Hebrew congregation became irritated and incensed by His doctrine. When Jews heard Paul saying that Jesus of Nazareth was the epitome of all they considered to be sacred, that He was the true Passover, they were dumbfounded! To exalt a carpenter to such realms of exaltation was unpardonable; the preacher should be silenced immediately. Yet, Paul continued to make his claim. He believed that what God had done in Egypt was a foreshadowing of what He intended to do for all mankind. What the lamb meant to the forefathers, Christ, the Lamb of God, was to all His followers. The apostle believed that the ancient feast had lost its significance and usefulness; it was a relic of history. Christ, the New Passover, would supply all that God's children would ever need.

*The effectiveness of His sacrifice*

The word translated "passover" was *pascha;* it meant *a passing over.* It was used to describe how God passed over the houses upon which had been sprinkled the blood of the slain lamb. Thereafter, it was used in connection with the institution which commemorated that event. The Passover was called the *paschal feast* and the offering *the paschal lamb.* Every Hebrew recognized that without the protective power of the blood, judgment would have fallen upon their ancestors. When Paul claimed that Jesus was *our* passover, he implied that what the lamb did for Israel, the blood of Christ did for the world. It had become the means of salvation for all who believed and obeyed God's command. The apostle believed Christ's message: "He that heareth my word, and believeth on him that sent me, hath everlasting life, *and shall not come into condemnation;* but is passed from death unto life" (John 5:24).

*The excitement of His survival*

It was easy for Jewish listeners to understand Paul's arguments, and their inability to refute his teaching increased their anger. The lambs which died in Egypt remained dead! Only memories accompanied the Hebrews on their journey toward Canaan. Every year the nation slew new lambs, but never on any occasion did an offering survive the sacrifice. Paul was exultant when he exclaimed: "But now is Christ risen from the dead, and become the firstfruits of them that slept'' (1 Cor. 15:20). If for no other reason than His resurrection, He was superior to any institution or sacrifice known in Israel. The Lamb of God had triumphed gloriously over death and was able to accompany His people on their pilgrimage to the Promised Land. He would be an ever-present help in the time of trouble and would be infinitely more to His followers than the paschal celebration ever was to Israel.

*The emphasizing of His statement*

God commanded Moses that the Passover should be perpetuated throughout all generations. ''And ye shall observe this thing for an ordinance to thee and to thy sons forever. And it shall come to pass, when ye be come to the land which the LORD will give you, according as he hath promised, that ye shall keep this service. And it shall come to pass, when your children shall say unto you, What mean ye by this service? that ye shall say, It is the sacrifice of the LORD'S passover, who passed over the houses of the children of Israel in Egypt, when he smote the Egyptians, and delivered our houses'' (Exod. 12:24-27). That command of God was faithfully observed. To perpetuate the knowledge of Christ and extend His kingdom, Christians should testify to families and friends. They should be thrilled with the privilege of communicating their faith to people who need to know about the Savior. Lights hidden ''under a bushel'' never shine in the darkness and are easily extinguished!

# LORD

(1 CORINTHIANS 12:3)

*Lord* was probably the most unique name ever given to the Savior. Writing to the church at Corinth, Paul declared: "Wherefore I give you to understand, that no man speaking by the Spirit of God, calleth Jesus accursed; and that no man can say that Jesus is Lord, but by the Holy Ghost." Paul believed it would be impossible for any person inspired by the Holy Spirit to curse the Savior. The apostle's second claim penetrated even more deeply into human consciousness. To call Jesus *Lord* implied that the Savior occupied the central place in the Christian's affections. Throughout the New Testament the people who called Christ by this name were those upon whom the Holy Spirit's power had fallen. He had opened the eyes of their understanding to see the indescribable beauty and majesty of their Master.

*The enlightened sinner (John 8:11)*

It was early morning when a guilty woman was dragged into the presence of Jesus. She had been caught in an act of adultery and had no excuse. Her accusers were merciless, and as they pressed their charges before the Stranger, it appeared she would soon be stoned to death. Then, the woman suddenly became aware of the reluctance of the Teacher to condemn her. She stared at Him and realized He was different from other men. When her accusers departed, she could not believe her eyes. Then she heard a voice of infinite tenderness asking, "Where are those thine accusers? Hath no man condemned thee? She said, No man, *Lord!*" Evidently the Holy Spirit was already opening the eyes of her understanding.

*The enemy. . . Saul (Acts 9:5)*

He was arrogant, ruthless, and without mercy. Yet he had suddenly been humiliated. He was lying in the dust, and his bewildered men were wondering what had happened to their courageous, determined leader. Then he heard a voice saying, "Saul, Saul, why persecutest thou me? And he said, Who art thou, *Lord?*" He hardly knew what was happening to him; he was a helpless man floundering amid his doubts and fears. He had lost his eyesight and was terrified and apprehensive. Later, he understood the impossibility of running away from God. Even at that early moment, the Holy Spirit was beginning to teach him a new language!

*The emotional Simon (Matt. 14:30)*

Peter was beginning to feel like a fool! His impetuosity had run away with his brains! Why had he left the boat to embark on such a stupid errand? He was sinking fast, he might even drown! Then, as the waves were about to close over his head, he saw Jesus and shouted, "*Lord,* save me. And immediately Jesus stretched forth his hand, and caught him, and said unto him, O thou of little faith." Thank God, he was back in the boat. Probably, his brothers were laughing. Now that the danger had passed, the incident was a cause for mirth. Did they realize the spontaneous cry "Lord" revealed an astonishing insight into the person of their Master?

*The earnest suppliant (Luke 23:42)*

Something strange and bewildering had taken place within the criminal who was dying. His fear and anger had disappeared. He no longer hated the soldiers who had driven spikes through his hands. There was something strange about the Man on the nearby cross. The inscription said that He was a king, the people said He was a blasphemer, but He was more! Then, suddenly, he understood and said unto Jesus, "*Lord,* remember me when thou comest into thy kingdom." That request changed his outlook. The Spirit of God had opened his eyes; he was safe!

*The enthralled saint (Acts 7:59)*

The crowd was hostile; their faces revealed the hatred which had destroyed their sanity. They were gathering stones, and death was imminent. Stephen was unafraid. He was going home! He lifted his eyes and beheld "the glory of God, and Jesus standing on the right hand of God. And he kneeled down, and cried with a loud voice, *Lord Jesus,* lay not this sin to their charge." The Savior had risen from His throne of splendor to give to the home-coming saint the greatest reception heaven could supply. There were no cataracts on the eyes of Stephen. To believe in Jesus was wonderful, but to know Him as *Lord* was even better!

# THE LAST ADAM

(1 CORINTHIANS 15:45)

The significance of this name only becomes apparent when it is contrasted with *the first Adam.* Jesus is never called the second, third, or fourth Adam. He was always *the Last Adam,* there could never be another. He was unique as the final representative sent by God to earth. The Lord came as a man to show humans how to live. Adam failed completely as the head of God's creation. An act of disobedience destroyed his purity; his example encouraged descendants to disobey the Almighty. As a result of his indiscretion, others were born in sin and eventually died. The Last Adam was tempted as was the first, but He survived the ordeal triumphantly (see Heb. 4:15). Jesus' righteousness enabled Him to impart eternal life to His followers so that they would never die! (See John 11:25-26.) The perfection of the Last Adam was God's answer to the imperfection of the first one.

PROPOSITION 1 . . . *The beginning and the end*

The first Adam began with everything and finished with nothing. The Last Adam began with nothing and finished with everything. The first man began his career as the head of the created world. Everything was subservient to him; his word controlled every creature. He was not subject to disease and death. Life could have been a long vacation. It was possible for him to live with his family amid scenes of enchanting beauty, but, alas, he ruined everything when he disobeyed his Creator. Finally, he left a legacy which enslaved his descendants. As a contrast to this unfortunate beginning, the Last Adam was born in a stable; His parents were poor. Yet, He became the greatest Benefactor to walk the earth. He conquered disease, devils, and death and established a kingdom which will last eternally.

PROPOSITION 2 . . . *The blessing and the endeavor*

The first Adam began with a commission to replenish the earth. The Last Adam began with a desire "to bring many sons to glory" and to fill a celestial city with redeemed people known as His bride. The first Adam needed *to live* in order to fulfill his obligations; the Second Adam had *to die* to make His dreams come true. His reconciling death atoned for humanity's sin and opened a highway to the heart of God. The first man allowed sin to pollute his nature; Jesus, although tempted as we are, remained sinless, and no attempt of the evil one spoiled the perfection of what He was and did.

PROPOSITION 3 . . . *The bride and the expense*

The first Adam was given a bride as a helpmate. She was a gift from God. The Last Adam had to purchase His Bride, and the cost was incalculable. Adam was placed into a deep sleep, and during his slumber God extracted that which was necessary for the creation of Eve. The Last Adam also was placed into the "deep sleep" of the Cross, and from the redemptive work thus accomplished, God arranged the creation of the Church. At the beginning of time, He married the first couple; at the end of time, the marriage of the Lamb will be the greatest festive event in the history of the universe. The bride will be presented to the Bridegroom, "without spot, or wrinkle, or any such thing."

PROPOSITION 4 . . . *The blessings in eternity*

The first Adam eventually lost his partner through age and death. The Last Adam will never be separated from His bride; they will share each other's company throughout eternity. There will never be any hospitals or nursing homes in heaven; cemeteries will not exist, while disease will be a very distant memory. "And there shall be no night there; and they need no candle, neither light of the sun; for the Lord God giveth them light" (Rev. 22:5). "They shall hunger no more, neither thirst any more. . . . For the Lamb which is in the midst of the throne shall feed them, and shall lead them unto living fountains of waters: and God shall wipe away all tears from their eyes" (Rev. 7:16-17). The poet was correct when he wrote,

> All that I need is in Jesus
> He satisfies, joy He supplies.

# A NAME ABOVE EVERY NAME

(PHILIPPIANS 2:6-9)

This remains the most inscrutable of all the names given to the Savior; no one but God knows what it is. Its importance is unlimited, its glory beyond comprehension, its beauty unsurpassed. God, who is omniscient and whose wisdom is unfathomable, decided to give His Son a special name to outshine in splendor all other names. People remember the Caesars and think of great conquests. Others remember Moses and meditate on the laws given to Israel. Rembrandt, Leonardo Da Vinci, and Michelangelo are associated with masterpieces of art. Mozart, Bach, and Handel bring to mind the greatest compositions in music. Edison and Marconi suggest discoveries which revolutionized communications. Meritorious achievements earned for these people great renown; each in his field was a genius. Jesus of Nazareth exceeded all of them. He founded an empire on love, and conquered enemies by the power of affection. As a constructor He built a bridge between the need of man and the sufficiency of God. As an artist He painted on human canvas the greatest portraits of God ever revealed to humanity. He recorded on the emotions of devoted listeners songs of liberty and joy which expressed the harmony of heaven. His exploits on behalf of heaven and earth so pleased the Almighty that God honored Christ with a special name—"*a name above every name.*"

*Far above all places (Eph. 4:8-10)*

"When Christ ascended up on high, he led captivity captive, and gave gifts unto men. Now that he ascended, what is it but that he also descended first into the lower parts of the earth? He that descended is the same also that ascended up *far above all heavens,* that he might fill all things." The universe in which we live is so vast that even the greatest telescopes can only probe the fringes of God's creation. Sir James Jeans said, "There are more worlds in space than there are grains of sand on all the beaches of earth." (*The Universe Around Us,* p. 12.) To gaze, even with the naked eye, at the star-filled heavens fascinates the mind. Scientists declare that there are suns in outer space which dwarf the sun that shines daily upon us. The immensity of the heavens beggars description and defies the efforts of men to unlock its undiscovered secrets. Yet, however great the heavens may be, Paul believed that his Savior was enthroned far above them all. It, therefore, became evident that when God chose a name for His matchless Son, it expressed the surpassing glory of excellence.

*Far above all persons (Heb. 1:3-4)*

When he commenced his letter to the Hebrews, the writer used eloquent terms to describe the eternal glories of the Savior, "who being the brightness of [God's] glory, and the express image of his person, and upholding all things by the word of his power, when he had by himself purged our sins, sat down on the right hand of the Majesty on high; being made *so much better than the angels,* as he hath by inheritance obtained *a more excellent name than they*" (Heb. 1:3-4). The Bible speaks of angels as being the servants of the living God and indicates that among their number are archangels, beings possessing greater wisdom, authority, and power. We are unable to explain all the intricacies of the angelic arrangement, but the Savior is greater than all. "He hath a *more excellent name* than they." The Bible describes elders around the throne of God and describes how they serve Him day and night in His temple. The unspecified splendor of that celestial scene may be beyond the powers of human comprehension.

*Far above all in preeminence (Col. 1:18)*

Writing to the Colossians, Paul said, "And he is the head of the body, the church; who is the beginning, the first born from the dead; that in all things he might have the preeminence." The Savior stands alone in magnificence. The greatest of earthly scholars bowed at His feet; the mightiest of human conquerors were overcome by His love; even kings joyfully became His subjects. The Savior, who possesses *the name above all names,* is best known through His love extended toward sinners.

# AN OFFERING AND A SACRIFICE TO GOD

(EPHESIANS 5:2)

When Paul described the Lord as "an offering and a sacrifice to God for a sweet smelling savor," he expressed the heart of the Christian gospel. He said more in one profound statement than other authors might have written in lengthy statements. Israel had always been accustomed to sacrifices on God's altar, but, probably, very few people understood their significance. Some made atonement; some deepened pity; others provided satisfaction and pleasure for Jehovah. It seems incomprehensible that whereas Christians looked at the cross and wept, God looked at it and smiled! It was for Him "a sweet smelling savor."

*Sacrifices had to be carefully chosen*

There are forty-three places in the Pentateuch where the patriarch emphasized that offerings should be *without blemish.* "Your lamb shall be without blemish" (Exod. 12:5). This requirement was also made concerning the priests who participated in the ceremonies. "Whosoever he be. . .that hath any blemish, let him not approach to offer the bread of his God. For whatsoever man he be that hath a blemish, he shall not approach: a blind man, or a lame, or he that hath a flat nose, or anything superfluous. . . No man that hath a blemish of the seed of Aaron the priest shall come nigh to offer the offerings of the LORD. . . ." (Lev. 21:17-21). When God chose His Son to be the supreme sacrifice, He chose absolute perfection.

*Sacrifices had to be officially offered*

Abraham offered his sacrifice upon Mount Moriah (Gen. 22:2), but throughout the history of Israel, people were required to take their offerings to the tabernacle or temple. Animals sacrificed elsewhere were only acceptable on very rare occasions. God was said to dwell above the mercy seat, while the blood of the offering had to be sprinkled *in His presence.* People who observed this requirement signified their allegiance to Jehovah and their obedience to His command. When the Lord was taken to Calvary, He went to the official place of execution; He was to die as God had appointed (see Deut. 21:22-23).

*Sacrifices had to be authentically accepted*

Priests examined every offering brought to the temple, and those found to be imperfect were rejected. Unfortunately, this custom was abused, and during the years of Christ's ministry, official inspectors rejected every offering unless it had been purchased in the markets owned by Caiaphas. Such abuse was denounced by Jesus, and those who participated in the infamous practice were driven from the temple (John 2:13-16). When the Lord Jesus offered Himself to God, the divine approbation became evident when He "was declared to be the Son of God with power, according to the spirit of holiness, by the resurrection from the dead" (Rom. 1:4). If the redeeming work of the Savior had been unacceptable to God, then Jesus would have remained in the grave.

*Sacrifices had to be individually identified*

Each sinner had to be identified with the offering in which he placed his trust. "And he shall put his hand upon the head of the burnt offering; and it shall be accepted for him to make atonement for him" (Lev. 1:4). There were occasions when the head of a household offered sacrifice for his family, but, basically, each offerer had to do so for himself. Identification was made when the sinner placed his hand upon the head of the animal to be slain; no man could do this for another. The same truth applies today. The death of Christ was truly the greatest sacrifice ever made, but unless a man identifies himself with that offering, he cannot be pardoned. No parent can be saved on behalf of his children, and no child can atone for his parent. The offer of God is personalized; each sinner must voluntarily by faith associate himself with Christ. When this is done, the sacrifice of the Lamb of God becomes a sweet-smelling savor unto God. It causes pleasure in heaven and unspeakable joy on earth.

# THE IMAGE OF THE INVISIBLE GOD. . .the Creator of all things

(COLOSSIANS 1:14-16)

It would be extremely interesting if it were possible to listen to Paul and John discussing theology. John wrote: "In the beginning was the Word, and the Word was with God, and the Word was God. . . .All things were made by him; and without him was not anything made that was made" (John 1:1, 3). Paul stated that the Lord was "the image of the invisible God. . .by him were all things created, that are in heaven, and that are in earth, by him all things consist" (Col. 1:15-17). Paul believed that Jesus is the image—that is, the living manifestation—of the eternal Father. He was *the one and only portrait of the Most High God.*

*How unlimited His power. . . "By him were all things created"*

To say the least, the scope of this magnificent revelation beggars description. John lived with the Savior and understood many things. Paul was a persecutor who, after his conversion, went into the desert to be instructed by the Holy Spirit. How and when this immense conception enlightened the minds of the two Christian leaders is unknown. Both men were convinced that Jesus existed before time began. He created the earth upon which He was crucified. His creative genius designed trees, flowers, and colors. He was the first to appreciate music and arranged that each little bird should contribute to the symphonies of praise to be heard in His world. It was not too difficult to turn water into wine at the wedding in Cana, for He had long since turned raindrops into rivers and moisture into oceans.

*How unique His portrait. . .the image of the invisible God*

Paul wrote to Timothy about the Almighty, "who is the blessed and only Potentate, the King of kings, and Lord of lords; who only hath immortality, *dwelling in the light which no man can approach unto; whom no man hath seen, nor can see:* to whom be honor and power everlasting. Amen" (1 Tim. 6:15-16). When Jehovah descended to Mount Sinai, the people were commanded to stay away so that they would not be consumed. Their leader, Moses, was given a limited vision of God. "And it shall come to pass, while my glory passeth by, that I will put thee in a cleft of the rock, and will cover thee with my hand while I pass by: and I will take away mine hand, and thou shalt see my back parts: but my face shall not be seen" (Exod. 33:22-23). Men have wondered what God is like, but as Paul and John reminisced, their questions were answered; God is like Jesus! The Savior's words suddenly assume new importance: "He that hath seen me hath seen the Father" (John 14:9).

*How unsurpassed His purpose . . . "To reconcile all things unto Himself"*

Christ had no problem bringing planets into being. He spoke and things were done! When the Lord created the universe, His powers were invincible; nothing was impossible. Yet, when the same Lord decided to create the Church, the task was indescribably different. The Savior planned "to reconcile all things unto himself" (Col. 1:20), but in order to do that, it was necessary "to make peace by the blood of his cross" (Col. 1:20). He took man's sin and carried it to the tree. God desired to destroy the hostility which separated humans. He wanted Jews and Samaritans to live together as brethren and all races to be at peace so that within the fold of the Great Shepherd, all should be His sheep. He desired a world without war, a planet without pain, a Church without prejudice. Yet, the price paid for such a possibility was high. The King had to leave His throne of splendor and descend to earth. Paul wrote, "And being found in fashion as a man, he humbled himself, and became obedient unto death, even the death of the cross. Wherefore, God also hath highly exalted him, and given him a name which is above every name" (Phil. 2:7-9). Jesus had seen a pearl of great value, and in His estimation no price was too high to obtain it (see Matt. 13:46).

# THE FIRST BEGOTTEN FROM THE DEAD

(COLOSSIANS 1:15, 18; ROMANS 8:29)

This profound name is among the most challenging ever given to the Savior; it embraced eternity! Throughout the ages, scholars have tried to comprehend its meaning, to fathom its depth, and to explain its inscrutable mysteries. The term, with variations, may be found in five places in the New Testament and the possibility exists that it will never be completely understood until time has ceased to be. The word translated "firstborn" is *prototokos* and W. E. Vine said: "It is used of Christ as born of the Virgin Mary (Luke 2:7), further, in His relationship to the Father, expressing His priority to, and preeminence over creation, but not in the sense of being the first to be born. It is used occasionally of *superiority of position.* The Old Testament counterpart of this word may be found in Exodus 4:22 and Deuteronomy 21:16-17." (*Expository Dictionary of Old and New Testament Words,* Vol. 2, p. 104).

*The Firstborn. . .preeminent in His position (Col. 1:15)*

Let it be admitted that finite minds are incapable of comprehending truth still veiled in eternal mists. The writer to the Hebrews stated, "And again when he bringeth in the first begotten into the world, he saith, Let all the angels of God worship him" (Heb. 1:6). It seems the divine presentation was made *after* the angels were created, for otherwise it would have been impossible for them to worship as they were directed. Many scholars have wrestled with this problem, but the consensus of opinion seems to be that, in the pre-creation ages, a decision was made that in dealings with the world to be, *God would manifest Himself in different ways.* Jehovah created new departments of activity! He would work through the Son and the Holy Spirit, and still remain as the Supreme Director of operations. He then appeared in a new form and to avoid confusion, commanded the angels to worship Him. The *Logos*—the Word—by whose power worlds had been created, is supreme in the universe and fills eternity with indescribable glory.

*The Firstborn. . .preeminent in His power (Col. 1:18)*

When the Son of God became Mary's *firstborn* child (Luke 2:7), once again He appeared in another form. He had existed from eternity but had never been conceived in a woman's womb (compare Mark 16:12). The Lord Jesus Christ was unique; He was creating something new—a highway from man's need to the sufficiency of heaven's resources. This became apparent when He rose triumphantly from the dead. Jesus was the first fruit of a great harvest. His victory was *complete, contagious,* and *convincing.* The apostle Paul wrote, "But now is Christ risen from the dead, and become the firstfruits of them that slept. . . .For as in Adam all die, even so in Christ shall all be made alive. But every man in his own order: Christ the firstfruits; afterward they that are Christ's at his coming" (1 Cor. 15:20, 22, 23). Even Job understood this glorious truth when he said, "For I know that my redeemer liveth, and that he shall stand at the latter day upon the earth: And though . . . *worms destroy this body,* yet in my flesh shall I see God: whom I shall see for myself, and mine eyes shall behold" (Job 19:25-27).

*The Firstborn . . .preeminent in His purpose (Rom. 8:29)*

Paul wrote, "For whom he did foreknow, he also did predestinate to be conformed to the image of his Son, that he might be the firstborn among many brethren." John wrote, "Beloved, now are we the sons of God, and it doth not yet appear what we shall be: but we know that, when he shall appear, we shall be like him; for we shall see him as he is" (1 John 3:2). The early Christians rejoiced in the fact they could share the Savior's triumph. They knew He had gone home to heaven and were convinced they would join Him in the eternal home. They remembered and preached His message: "I am the resurrection and the life; he that believeth in me, though he were dead, yet shall he live: And whosoever liveth and believeth in me shall never die" (John 11:25-26). Jesus was the *First Fruits* of the new creation, the Church, to appear in heaven. Thereafter, He was ready to welcome His beloved followers when they reached the end of their earthly pilgrimage.

# THE HEAD OF THE BODY . . . the Church

(COLOSSIANS 1:18)

Paul's first chapter in his letter to the Colossians remains unsurpassed for beauty of expression, depth of theology, and effectiveness in presenting truth. His range of thought spans time and reaches into eternity. It transcends all earthly things and penetrates the highest heaven. Paul wrote, "[Christ] is the image of the invisible God, the firstborn of every creature: For by him were all things created, that are in heaven, and that are in earth, visible and invisible, whether they be thrones, or dominions, or principalities, or powers: all things were created by him, and for him: and he is before all things, and by him all things consist. And he is the head of the body, the church: who is the beginning, the firstborn from the dead; that in all things he might have the preeminence. For it pleased the Father that in him should all fulness dwell" (Col. 1:15-19). The apostle was thrilled to announce that He who had been present in eternity had created something new! The planets, stars, and millions of worlds in space were the result of His creative genius, but what had been accomplished through redemption surpassed anything previously known.

*The head is indispensable*

No body can exist without its head! No church can exist without Christ! Every blessing known in this life comes from God (see James 1:17). Christ, the Head of the Church, planned, perfected, provided, and still preserves our salvation. Without Him, all humanity would be bankrupt! The foundation upon which His new work rested was "redemption through his blood, even the forgiveness of sins" (Col. 1:14). The means by which the project was perfected and strengthened was that "He became the firstborn from the dead." He rose again to complete what He had commenced. Through the ministry of the Holy Spirit, men and women were being built into a "holy temple for the Lord." Jesus had become the Head of a spiritual body, the presiding Head of His new creation—*the Church of the living God.* To Him, all His followers would look for guidance; from Him, His people would expect assistance; and to Him, all subjects would render loyal service. Jesus deserved preeminence in all things.

*The head is intelligent*

The brain is the nerve center of every intelligent human action. When the mind ceases to function, the body becomes useless. The president of any business is responsible for everything which takes place among his subordinates. Success or failure in every enterprise depends upon the efficiency of the man who directs operations. The same might be claimed of the Head of the Church. His amazing work earned His place at the right hand of God. The Savior was able to say to His Father, "I have glorified thee on the earth; I have finished the work thou gavest me to do" (John 17:4). God responded by saying, "Sit on my right hand, until I make thine enemies thy footstool" (Heb. 1:13). To repeat what has already been suggested, Christ sits at the nerve center of every action inspired by God; He plans and directs activities, and therefore, His subjects should be careful to seek His guidance before embarking on any project relative to the extension of His kingdom.

*The head is inter-related*

Without a head, a body is useless; but it is also true to say that the Lord depends on us. The head conceives a plan, but the members of the body supply the means whereby that plan becomes operative. More often than not, a person whose body is paralyzed stays in a wheelchair. When the members of the body of Christ do not function, frustration fills the heart of God. The Lord Jesus is dependent upon the members of His body to extend His Kingdom. If the original disciples had failed to fulfill their commission to evangelize the world, the gospel would have remained in Palestine. If Paul had become a parochial priest, millions of Gentiles would not have heard His message. The apostles did not fail in their task; neither should we. Since we owe everything to the Head of the Church, we cannot do too much for Him. Concerning Christ and His Church it might be said, "United we stand; divided we fall."

# THE HEIR OF ALL THINGS

(HEBREWS 1:2)

Let it be admitted that little is known of the far-reaching immensity of the amazing statement about Jesus' all-inclusive inheritance; "all things" are *all things,* "whether they be things in earth, or things in heaven!" (Col. 1:20). "For by him were all things created, that are in heaven, and that are in earth, visible and invisible, whether they be thrones, or dominions, or principalities, or powers: all things were created by him, and for him: and he is before all things, and by him all things consist" (Col. 1:16-17). Men are beginning to explore the fringes of outer space, but even the most brilliant scientist can only speculate as to what exists in the celestial worlds. It is hoped that discoveries will be made which will revolutionize medical and industrial research, but at the present time the heavens are shrouded in mystery. Men know only a little about the universe in which they live. Long ago Paul said, "All things were made by him, and for him." The writer to the Hebrews, who might also have been Paul, exclaimed, "God. . .hath in these last days, spoken unto us by his Son, *whom he hath appointed heir of all things*" (Heb. 1:2).

*An appointed inheritance*

The principle, "Give and it shall be given unto you," operates in every sphere. It is impossible to outgive God, for He has many ways to pay His debts and reward faithful service. The laws which were given to men also applied in heaven. God gave work to His Son, and it was a moment of glorious ecstasy when the Savior was able to say, "I have glorified thee on the earth: I have finished the work which thou gavest me to do" (John 17:4). Even David recognized this truth when he said, "The Lord said unto my Lord, Sit thou at my right hand, until I make thine enemies thy footstool" (Ps. 110:1). It became evident that before time commenced, God desired His Son to become the recipient of heaven's greatest award. Jesus, who was the image of the invisible God, was meant to be Lord of His own creation. It was planned that way, and what God decrees always comes to pass.

*An acknowledged inheritance (Mark 12:7)*

The illustrations given by the Lord were significant; they expressed His thoughts. The parable of the vineyard was an outstanding example of this fact. He spoke of a husbandman who sent his servants at harvest time to collect dues. When they were treated shamefully, the lord of the vineyard sent his son. When this became known to the workmen, they said, "This is the heir; come, let us kill him, and the inheritance shall be ours." That account revealed that the Savior was aware of His destiny and realized He would inherit everything His Father owned. Jesus was able to see the end from the beginning and knew exactly what would transpire at the end of time. The implications of that parable and others are unmistakable.

*An abandoned inheritance (1 Cor. 15:28)*

Writing of future events, Paul declared, "And when all things shall be subdued unto him, then shall the Son also himself be subject unto him that put all things under him, that God may be all in all." The apostle had already revealed, "The last enemy that shall be destroyed is death" (1 Cor. 15:26), and therefore the submission of the Son to the Father had to be the climax of the Lord's magnificent labor. It would be within His legal right to occupy a throne of splendor and rule over God's immense universe. That privilege He will reject in order to do something else. The Lord will abdicate His throne in order to marry His bride—the Church. At that time, the marriage of the Lamb will become a reality. Paul expounded this truth when he wrote to the Ephesians, saying, "Christ also loved the church, and gave himself for it . . . that he might present it to himself a glorious church, not having spot, or wrinkle, or any such thing; that it should be holy and without blemish" (Eph. 5:25-27). Christ's love for His bride will surpass everything else. Willingly, He will share His inheritance, so that through endless ages, He and His beloved might enjoy unbroken, unending fellowship. That truth was probably the greatest revelation ever given by God to men. (See 1 Cor. 15:28.)

# THE FAITHFUL APOSTLE

(HEBREWS 3:1)

The Greek word *apostolos* means "one who is sent." It was used to express the relationship between Christ and His Father (Heb. 3:1). The disciples were so called to indicate they were chosen by Jesus to be sent forth on preaching missions (Luke 6:13). Paul, although he was not one of the original twelve, was commissioned by the Lord and became the apostle to the Gentiles (Acts 22:21). Apparently, within the New Testament the word had a wider meaning, for Barnabas was also called an apostle—a sent one (Acts 14:14). Two unnamed Christians were also mentioned as being special messengers dispatched by the churches (2 Cor. 8:23). It must, therefore, be considered that the term "apostles" should not be considered an indication of eminence within the church. It expressed the privilege of *selection.*

*He was a reliable Messenger . . . He never avoided His duty*

It is significant that Paul mentioned "false apostles" (*pseudapostolos*) (2 Cor. 11:13). The reliability of the Lord is best appreciated when contrasted with those other messengers. A few of God's chosen servants turned from their path of duty by endeavoring to reach places where they could not be found. Jonah, for example, made a sea journey which took him out of the will of God and close to disaster. Jesus, although beset by many problems and foes, never deviated from His assigned path, and that was one of the reasons why God said, "This is my beloved Son, in whom I am well pleased: *hear ye Him*" (Matt. 17:5).

*He was a resourceful Messenger . . . He knew what to do*

The scribes and Pharisees brought to Jesus a woman who had been caught in an act of adultery. The question they asked was designed to make the Lord commit Himself to a specific course of action. If He had said, "Stone her," they would have done so to discredit His message of love. Had He said, "Do not stone her," they would have arrested Him on a charge of breaking the law. Therefore, Jesus refused to supply an answer until He had considered every aspect of the situation. When, eventually, He replied, His tempters were dumbfounded.

*He was a relentless Messenger . . . He never avoided responsibilities*

Many of His early followers turned away when danger threatened; some of His closest associates became conspicuous by their absence. Yet, Jesus never tried to avoid the task given by His Father. Luke described how the Samaritans refused to welcome Him "because his face was as though he would go to Jerusalem" (see Luke 9:53). The Savior was determined to follow the appointed way, although to do so led to death.

*He was a remarkable Messenger . . . He never failed*

This claim could not have been made of any other New Testament preacher. Elisha, who was indisputably a type of Christ, asked for a double portion of the Holy Spirit, and there was no record of failure in his ministry. Similarly, the Lord endured every trial, offset every temptation, and eventually exclaimed triumphantly, "It is finished" (John 19:30).

*He was a resplendent Messenger . . . His face and garments shone*

Recalling what had happened in the Mount of Transfiguration, Matthew wrote, "And Jesus was transfigured before them: and his face did shine as the sun, and his raiment was white as the light" (Matt. 17:2). The intrinsic beauty of the Lord could not be completely hidden, the glory which He shared with God from the dawn of time was always within His breast, and there were moments when the frail barrier of flesh could not hold back that which demanded expression. When John was permitted to see the Lord standing between the lampstands, he was astonished and later wrote, "His head and his hairs were white like wool; and his eyes were as a flame of fire" (Rev. 1:14). The Lord Jesus Christ was the most wonderful Apostle or Courier ever commissioned by God. Wise are they who receive His message.

# THE AUTHOR AND FINISHER OF OUR FAITH

(HEBREWS 5:9)

The fact that Jesus is called an "author" is truly significant, for He never wrote a book, and the Bible only mentions one occasion when He wrote anything (John 8:6-8). Obviously Christ read the Scriptures, for His sermons contained references to the writings of the prophets. He inspired prophets to write books and has blessed innumerable authors, but the fact remains the Lord never published a book or wrote an article. The writer of the Epistle to the Hebrews refers to Him as "the author and finisher of our faith" (12:2) and the term "author" in that connection evidently means *the beginner, the originator, the one responsible for the commencement.*

*An author discerns . . . he knows!*

Every writer has something to say! He has a story in his mind and sees the end from the beginning. With carefully chosen words, he describes what has been considered and finally produces a book which never existed earlier. It is evident that the Lord had something to say. There existed in His mind the greatest story ever to be told; it stretched from eternity to eternity, from the heights of heaven's magnificence to the depth of human degradation. It was a glorious unfolding of love beyond comprehension and an account of the death and resurrection of a Prince who was willing to die for sinners. His book had a wonderful ending!

*An author deliberates . . . he thinks!*

The writer to the Hebrews said, "For it became him . . . in bringing many sons unto glory, to make the captain of their salvation perfect through sufferings" (2:10). The word *archeegos,* translated "captain," really meant "author", and His story revealed the method by which He planned to accomplish this tremendous work. He considered the immensity of the project and decided how His secret should be revealed (see Heb. 9:1-10 and Eph. 3:5). That the glorious gospel was known in eternal ages was made clear by John's remarkable statement that his Master was "the Lamb slain from the foundation of the world" (Rev. 13:8).

*An author describes . . . he writes!*

Jesus is said to be "the author of eternal salvation" (Heb. 5:9) and "the author and finisher of our faith" (Heb. 12:2). Each of these two themes belongs to the other. The gospel cannot be of much use unless its truth is grasped by the hand of faith. Similarly, faith is of little use unless it sees something to grasp! A drowning man may believe that a lifebelt can prevent his drowning, but if he refuses to grasp it, he might sink beneath the waves. These truths had to be explained to needy people, and therefore, the Author of both the gospel and the capacity to comprehend its message, prepared a volume for potential readers. He chose human pens with which to write, and finally the manuscript was completed. There will never be an effective substitute for the Bible; this was the Book planned in heaven.

*An author delights . . . when his book is in demand*

People who seldom read never learn. Some of the greatest books ever written are seldom if ever read. God's Book, which describes how to find eternal treasure, is often within the reach of impoverished souls, but alas, the priceless volume is left to gather dust on a shelf. They who close their eyes should never complain of the dark! Those who turn their backs on God should never complain of their inability to see His face! Jesus was *the Author, the Beginner, the One who caused things to happen;* yet, even He can do little if men refuse to listen, to read, to understand what He says. The divine Author provided a road map to assist travelers on the journey to the celestial city. Blessed is the man who consults it every day.

# THE TESTATOR

(HEBREWS 9:16-17)

The writer of the Letter to the Hebrews was evidently a Jew well versed in the Scripture and acquainted with temple ritual. His thesis compared and contrasted past and present forms of worship to prove that the new covenant of grace was better than the old covenant based on legalism. The former at its best was restrictive; the new arrangement was redemptive, resplendent, and remarkable. It reached down to the depth of human depravity, out to all nations, and upward toward the heart of God. It was conceived in eternity, completed on Calvary's hill, and ratified in heaven. It was planned and perfected by the Prince of Peace, the great Testator, who revealed to impoverished sinners the way by which they could share an eternal inheritance. Paul expressed the same truth in his letter to the Ephesians. The apostle's progression of thought is exciting. He said that Christ is the One (1) "*In whom* we have redemption through his blood" (Eph. 1:7), (2) "*In whom* we have an inheritance" (Eph. 1:11), (3) "*In whom* ye were sealed" (Eph. 1:13), (4) "*In whom* ye are builded" (Eph. 2:22), and (5) "*In whom* we have boldness" (Eph. 3:12). All this was part of the inheritance bequeathed by heaven's Testator to those mentioned in His last will and testament.

*An inheritance implies that somebody is wealthy*

"For where there is a last will and testament involved, the death of the one who made it must be established. For a will and testament is valid and takes effect only at death, since it has no force or legal power as long as the one who made it is alive" (*The Amplified New Testament,* p. 845). A penniless beggar could never bequeath anything except rags! If a person owns property or anything else of value, that man or woman may bequeath all or part of his estate to whomever he chooses. When Paul wrote, "In whom also we have obtained an inheritance," he implied that the Savior possesses something which He desires to share with beneficiaries. To do this, He made His last will and testament, in which He stated clearly that His eternal possessions should be shared by all His followers. That inheritance was described in various ways, but Paul described it best in 2 Corinthians 8:9, "For ye know the grace of our Lord Jesus Christ, that, though he was rich, yet for your sakes he became poor, that ye through his poverty might become rich."

*It is death that validates a will*

"For a testament is of force after men are dead; otherwise it is of no strength at all while the testator liveth." It is thrilling to know that the Lord thought of sinners long before Adam was created. "He hath chosen us in him before the foundation of the world'' (Eph. 1:4). Yet, if the Testator had remained in heaven, that great document would have been invalid. It expressed only a thought in the mind of God. When the Lord died, His last will and testament became operative. Jesus satisfied every requirement of heaven's law and fulfilled what had been planned in eternity. When Jesus rose from the dead, He became His own executor. There was no need to appoint any friend, relative, or bank to superintend the administration of His estate; the Lord reserved that privilege for Himself.

*No inheritance is of value unless it is claimed*

A man could die of malnutrition while great riches awaited him in a bank. It is foolish to have millions of dollars in an account if the person has neither money in his pocket nor food in his stomach. What has been provided by a gracious benefactor must be claimed. Paul asserted that God had provided pardon for sins, fellowship for loneliness, promises to banish doubt, the indwelling Holy Spirit to replace weakness with divine strength, and an eternal home for every follower of the Lord Jesus Christ. This represented eternal wealth, something which surpassed the resources of earth. Yet, none of God's preparation would avail if the sinner did not claim his inheritance. Even a casual reading of the Epistle to the Hebrews reveals that all this was in the mind of the writer. He knew the Testator and desired that everyone know of the possibility of sharing in Christ's eternal estate.

# AN HIGH PRIEST OVER THE HOUSE OF GOD

(HEBREWS 10:21)

To sit at the side of a king or president is a very great honor, and few of the inhabitants of earth ever attain to such exaltation. To sit on the *right-hand side* of a ruler is an even greater honor. It is of increasing interest that the Epistle to the Hebrews emphasizes that Christ is seated at the right hand of the Majesty on high. This was the greatest honor God could confer upon His Son. The work given to Him had been completed; the job was finished. When the Almighty crowned Christ with glory and honor, He expressed complete satisfaction with everything which had been done during the ministry of Jesus upon the earth. The coronation scene in heaven surely beggared description (see Heb. 2:9).

*Christ's rightful place (Heb. 1:3 and 1:13)*

Hebrews 1:8 reveals that Jesus was not an ordinary man. He was from eternity and was divine. The Jews said of Him, "This man maketh himself *equal with God,"* and the Lord never denied the accusation, for it was true. He *did* make Himself equal with God. It is of the utmost importance to recognize that even God admitted this. The law explicitly stated that worship was to be rendered to God alone. Yet, in Hebrews 1:6 we are told that the Almighty commanded that even the angels should worship the Son, who was the expression of deity (v. 13), the Creator of the worlds (v. 2). When the Savior returned to the right hand of God, He was going home! He belonged there! If for no other reason, we must acknowledge that the Lord is a Priest with whom no other can compare.

*Christ's royal place (Heb. 8:1)*

Apart from the mysterious Melchizedek, there was never any *royal priest.* His royalty expresses power and His priesthood, concern for those He represents. Christ speaks and acts with *authority.* Seated far above principalities and powers, He intercedes for His own. His hand is upon the eternal throne, but His heart belongs to His followers. He was and is still a Priest after the order of Melchizedek, the king of Salem. Salem means "peace" and Christ is our peace. There is no need to be alarmed; the Lord is our Savior, Friend, and High Priest at the throne of the living God.

*His redemptive place (Heb. 10:12)*

It is helpful to read John 20:7 and to realize that, on the first Easter morning, Jesus made a visit to heaven. Doubtless, He went to present His credentials before the Father. It is thought-provoking for us to consider that never in the Gospel records was Christ presented as the High Priest of His people. First, the Lamb had to be offered, and then the priest began his work of intercession. Mary was told not to touch the Lord because Calvary had changed the Savior (John 20:17). He was about to do more for His followers than had ever been previously attempted. He had atoned for sin by the merits of His sacrifice, an action that provided priestly credentials. The *throne of judgment* was about to become *a throne of grace.*

*His radiant place (Heb. 12:2)*

Christ never tried to avoid what men might have called "the ultimate tragedy." When He contemplated His crucifixion, He was thrilled with joy. If we may use modern terms, He had graduated from the school of preparation and was ready to become an attorney! The fact that millions of people would soon seek His services filled Him with ecstasy. Men and women should always look to Jesus. He was present when our conversion experience began; He will be there eternally. "Having therefore, brethren, boldness to enter into the holiest by the blood of Jesus, by a new and living way, which he hath consecrated for us, through the veil, that is to say, his flesh; and having a high priest over the household of God; let us draw near with a true heart in full assurance of faith" (Heb. 10:19-22).

The effectiveness of the Aaronic priesthood was severely limited in that the officials were "not suffered to continue by reason of death." There were numerous high priests, each succeeding his predecessor. "But this man, because he continueth ever, hath an unchangeable priesthood" (see Heb. 7:23-24). He is always "on duty," and His arms are extended toward His clients!

# THE REWARDER OF FAITH

(HEBREWS 11:6)

Since the beginning of time people have been aware of work and wages, merit and reward. It is, therefore, no cause for amazement that throughout the Bible references can be found to illustrate this fact. Joseph was elevated to a position of regal importance in Egypt because he gave aid and advice to Pharaoh (Gen. 41:39-40). The Shunammite woman was blessed and protected during a famine because she was kind to a prophet (2 Kings 4:10; 8:1-6). The family of Obededom prospered exceedingly because he welcomed the ark of God into his home (2 Sam. 6:10-11). When Jesus taught in Palestine, He told a story of a lord who said to a servant, "Well done, thou good and faithful servant; thou hast been faithful over a few things, I will make thee ruler over many things" (Matt. 25:21). Evidently, God is aware of faithful service.

PROPOSITION 1. . . *Merit is always rewarded*

Paul wrote to the Corinthians regarding events to take place at the judgment seat of Christ. He said, "For other foundation can no man lay than that is laid, which is Jesus Christ. Now if any man build upon this foundation, gold, silver, precious stones. . . *he shall receive a reward*" (1 Cor. 3:11-14). Salvation is a gift from God, but eternal rewards must be earned by faithful service. Whatever is conscientiously done for the Savior cannot remain unnoticed. The Lord said, "And whosoever shall give to drink unto one of these little ones a cup of cold water only in the name of a disciple, verily I say unto you, he shall in no wise lose his reward" (Matt. 10:42). Often, the joy of helping another is in itself the most satisfactory reward possible. Nevertheless, Jesus taught that everything attempted for God will be officially recognized and rewarded when saints appear before their Lord (see Luke 14:14).

PROPOSITION 2. . . *Greater service wins greater rewards*

The Bible teaches that some awards will be greater than others. When Jesus spoke of persecution to be expected by His followers, He said, "Rejoice, and be exceeding glad: for *great* is your reward in heaven" (Matt. 5:12). He also promised special recognition for those who loved their enemies. "But love ye your enemies. . . and your reward shall be *great*" (Luke 6:35). The writer to the Hebrews was aware of the problems confronting his readers and was concerned lest they should lose their faith. He wrote, "Cast not away therefore your confidence, which hath *great* recompense of reward" (Heb. 10:35). The rewards to be given to the Christians will be decided by the quality of service rendered during their sojourn on earth. God expects the best from His children. Half-hearted, unenthusiastic effort can only be a source of disappointment. Although the believer in Christ cannot lose his eternal life (John 10:28), he may lose his crown (Rev. 3:11). Workmen who sleep on their job may lose many things. Soldiers who sleep at their post are in great danger.

PROPOSITION 3. . . *It is possible to win a full reward*

The *Amplified Version* of the New Testament supplies a very interesting translation of 2 John 8. "Take care; look to yourselves that ye may not lose [throw away or destroy] all that we, and you have labored for, but that you may [persevere until you] win, and receive back *a perfect reward—-in full.*" Commenting on this scripture, Jamieson, Fausset, and Brown, say, "There are degrees of heavenly reward proportioned to the degrees of capability of receiving heavenly blessedness. Each vessel of glory hanging on Jesus shall be fully happy." There are *rewards, great rewards,* and a *full reward.* All workers for Christ should ascertain whether or not they are doing their utmost for the Savior. Paul gave excellent advice when in writing to the Galatians, he said, "And let us not be weary in well doing: for in due season we shall reap, if we faint not" (Gal. 6:9). It will be wonderful to hear the Lord Jesus saying, "Well done, thou good and faithful servant. . .enter thou into the joy of thy Lord" (see Matt. 25:21). Christians have an excellent Master, a glorious opportunity, and an inestimable privilege.

# THE HELPER

(HEBREWS 13:6)

The writer to the Hebrews gave remarkable advice to his readers. He also gave to Jesus a name, which, though not sensational, expresses the faith of millions of Christians. He recommended procedures which would enable them to proclaim triumphantly, "The Lord is my Helper." This might have been a reference to the psalmist, who said: "The Lord *is on my side* [*is for me*]; *I will not fear: what can man do unto me?*" (Ps. 118:6). The psalmist had known bitter experiences when friends deserted him, circumstances threatened, and the future seemed foreboding and bleak. Then the light of the divine Presence became evident, and as the despondent man watched, his gloom was replaced by the dawn of a new day of encouragement. God came to his rescue, and songs of deliverance replaced sighs of despair.

Many years later, the man who wrote to the Hebrews knew similar experiences and was able to encourage those who were suffering. He urged them to live exemplary lives rather than to covet the wealth of their neighbors and to be calm, serene, and prayerful. Their motto should be "The Lord is my Helper."

*A compassionate Helper (Rom. 8:26)*

The letter sent by Paul to the Roman church expressed some of the greatest truths in the New Testament. Paul had plumbed the depths and scaled the heights of Christian experience; he knew both the sadness of despair and the thrill of success. He had suffered adversity, and his writings echoed his experiences. Perhaps the truth which strengthened him most was expressed in Romans 8:26: "Likewise the Spirit also *helpeth our infirmities:* for we know not what we should pray for as we ought." The apostle had probably known occasions when emotion effectively silenced his voice and when even prayer became impossible. Sorrow, frustration, disappointment, and failure to overcome evil can all depress a Christian. Paul was able to announce that during such times, the Spirit of God could assume control over everything—even prayer. The apostle knew he had two Intercessors, one at God's right hand, and the Other close at hand!

*A constant Helper (Ps. 46:1)*

The psalmist exclaimed, "God is our refuge and strength, *a very present help* in trouble." This was one of the most eloquent statements ever made by the sweet singer of Israel. A helper is always a friend, but, unfortunately, some who would give assistance are not close enough to do so. Job felt lonely and afraid when he believed God had forgotten him. He needed help urgently but could only say,

"Oh that I knew where I might find him that I might come even to his seat!" (Job 23:2). Paul knew, as did the psalmist, that God is never far from those who trust in Him. At any time of the day or night, in any place, and in all circumstances, the Lord could be the Helper of His people.

*A confident Helper (Isa. 41:13)*

Isaiah lived in troubled times, and it was, therefore, reassuring when God said, "For I the LORD thy God will hold thy right hand, saying unto thee, Fear not. . . I will help thee. . . . I will open rivers in high places, and fountains in the midst of the valleys: I will make the wilderness a pool of water, and the dry land springs of water. . . . that they may see, and know, and consider, and understand together, that the hand of the LORD hath done this. . . ." (Isa. 41:13, 14, 18, 20). The magnificent range of help promised by God is almost beyond comprehension. He is capable of doing anything!

*A conditional Helper (Heb. 4:16)*

The Lord Jesus Christ was the channel through whom blessings came to men. His ministry did not end when He returned to heaven. He interceded for His people before the throne of God and was able to continue assisting those who diligently sought Him. Nevertheless, there was a condition which needed to be considered. He expected His followers to seek the help which was possible. The ancient writer reminded the New Testament Christians of this important fact. "Let us therefore come boldly unto the throne of grace, that we may obtain mercy, and find grace to help in time of need." People who never walk the road of prayer never find jewels along the way. Christians who never look up never see the stars!

# THE MEDIATOR

(1 TIMOTHY 2:5)

Many of the names given to the Savior appear to be synonymous. They are so alike that, at first glance, it is difficult to detect any difference between them. They resemble snowflakes, each extremely delicate and beautiful, and yet when examined closely, every flake is an original masterpiece of divine art. Christ has been called Intercessor, High Priest, Advocate, and Mediator: and all these names relate to His mediatorial work at the throne of God in heaven. To change the simile, they are glittering facets of a scintillating diamond. Each shining surface of resplendence possesses exquisite areas of beauty which await discovery by thoughtful students of the Bible. The name *Mediator* is an outstanding example of this fact.

*The irreconcilable resistancies*

The *Reader's Digest Encyclopedic Dictionary* states that a mediator is appointed "to act between disputing parties in order to bring about a settlement." A priest intercedes, a lawyer or advocate defends, an intercessor prays, but a mediator is a go-between for two parties beyond reconciliation. Governments appoint such men to arbitrate between opposing sections in an industrial dispute. When employers and employees refuse to accept viewpoints other than their own, a mediator is expected to produce an agreement acceptable to both, and the task is often exceedingly difficult. Referring to God, Job said, "For he is not a man as I am, that I should answer him, and we should come together in judgment. Neither is there any daysman betwixt us, *that might lay his hand upon us both*" (Job 9:32-33). The word translated "daysman" means *mediator* or *umpire.* An umpire is an impartial judge whose services make games possible. Sometimes, these officials are not popular, but without them no athletic contest would be successful. The Bible teaches that God and the human race are not in agreement; their respective demands are in opposition. God requires people to be holy, but they love to be sinful. This was clearly revealed by Christ in the parable where citizens said, "We will not have this man to reign over us" (see Luke 19:14). Like Job, humans need a "daysman" to resolve the problems between heaven and earth.

*The irreplaceable Representative*

Paul wrote to Timothy, "For there is one God, and one mediator between God and man, the man Christ Jesus" (1 Tim. 2:5). The quality of impartiality must be paramount in every mediator. For example, the Savior must fully represent the interests of both God and humanity. Favoritism can never be permitted, for each and every agreement must be ratified in righteousness. Christ must enjoy the complete confidence of both sides in the dispute, so that what He decides will never again be contested. His own impeccable holiness could never be questioned, and His love for both sides in the dispute was the guarantee of a genuine solution. Jesus earned the right to represent men and women; He died for them. He also was worthy of heaven, for He was an accredited member of the Trinity. No other person possessed such credentials; no other had such outstanding ability to solve difficult problems. Without the work of the Lord Jesus Christ, human beings would not even be permitted to enter into the presence of God. The help of the Mediator was indispensable.

*The indisputable results*

The writer to the Hebrews stated the Lord was the Mediator of a *better covenant* (Heb. 8:6) and a *new testament* (Heb. 9:15; 12:24). He also itemized some of the details of the arrangement which had been ratified by heaven and earth. "And for this cause he is the mediator of the new testament, that by means of death, for the redemption of the transgressions that were under the first testament, they which are called might receive the promise of eternal inheritance" (Heb. 9:15). No man can deny that the Mediator negotiated a "better covenant" for the human race. Redemption through His death and resurrection was followed by the glorious certainty of enjoying eternal life. We may not comprehend all that might be included in "an eternal inheritance," but it evidently includes receiving from God that which He alone can give. The relationship known by Moses cannot compare with what was obtained for us by the mediatorial services of our Lord.

Yesterday He helped me,<br>
Today, He did the same:<br>
How long will this continue?<br>
Forever, Praise His Name.

# THE BISHOP AND GUARDIAN OF SOULS

(1 Peter 2:25)

This intriguing name is remarkable for its ecclesiastical connotation. The Greek word *episkopon* has been translated "bishop," and it suggests *an official* who has oversight over others. The other word in the text is *poimena,* which means "a shepherd." Evidently, the terms are interrelated. The shepherd cares for his flock and leads his sheep to green pastures and still waters. The bishop or guardian of the flock exhibits courage in that he is ready at any moment to protect those for whom he is responsible. A bishop of the church is a man of authority able to discipline the rebellious, correct the faulty, and help those whose inexperience makes them inadequate to meet the demands of their calling. He is capable of making decisions and interpreting the commands of a higher authority. To him, ministers look for guidance and expect from him an example of efficiency. When Peter called the Lord the *bishop* or *guardian* of souls, he may have been thinking of events within his own lifetime.

*His relationship to the worker*

Commenting on the title "The Bishop of Your Souls," Adam Clarke, the famous expositor, writes, "Unless we consider the word 'bishop' to be a corruption of *episcopus,* and that this literally means *an overseer; an inspector;* or *one that has the oversight:* it can convey to us no meaning of the original. Jesus Christ is the Overseer of souls. He has them continually under His eye; He knows their wants, wishes, and dangers, and provides for them" (*The Bethany Parallel Commentary of the New Testament,* p. 1377). Within the church, a bishop is closely related to curates, vicars, and other ecclesiastical officials. He knows where each man or woman works and is acquainted with the possibilities and problems of each parish. If he has supervision over institutions, schools, or convalescent hospitals, he is aware of the problems of the staff and is ready to help in every emergency. Peter probably thought of these facts when he wrote his epistle. The Savior was not far away in heaven, but nearby watching, caring, and waiting to help His friends. As a shepherd led the sheep, so the Bishop led his organization. No worker should despair when such a Benefactor was near. The Bishop and the workman should share each other's problems.

*His regard for the work*

The Bishop's interest in the worker is equalled only by His enthusiasm for the progress of the work. At all times, the quality of both work and worker would be preeminent. Any pastor, minister, or official can be dismissed if he does not perform satisfactorily.

The project in hand is the strengthening of the church and the evangelizing of the world. A man who puts his hand to the plough should never look back (see Luke 9:62). As the Shepherd, the Savior loves His sheep, but as the Bishop, He disciplines His followers if their conduct threatens the safety and health of others. This undeniable fact is an encouragement and a warning to every worker within the church of Christ. They are never to be complacent or satisfied. Much work remains to be done, and the Lord is dependent upon His followers to complete what had been commenced.

*His reward for well-doing*

Within an organization, it is not wise to irritate or anger a superior. He has the ability to promote or demote any under his supervision and can either help or hinder the progress of a lesser official. Simon Peter was aware of this important fact. If an individual or a church did not perform to the expectation of the Lord, "his candlestick, or lampstand," might be removed (see Rev. 2:5). The positive side of this truth was expressed when the writer to the Hebrews said, "For God is not unrighteous to forget your work and labor of love, which ye have shewed toward his name, in that ye have ministered to the saints, and do minister" (Heb. 6:10). The Bishop of souls said, "And thou shalt be blessed . . . for thou shalt be recompensed at the resurrection of the just" (Luke 14:14). Any worker who values material gain more than spiritual wealth advertises his folly!

# AN ADVOCATE

(1 JOHN 2:1)

Advocate was an unusual name derived from a Greek word usually translated "comforter." For example, the Lord said, "And I will pray the Father, and he shall give you another *Comforter,* that he may abide with you for ever" (John 14:16). The word meant "one who comes alongside to help." Nevertheless, Dr. George R. Berry, the professor of Semitic languages in the University of Chicago, stated that its primary meaning is *an advocate* or *an intercessor* (see *The Greek-English Lexicon,* p. 75). Although the high priest of Israel interceded for his people, his primary duty was to sprinkle the blood of sacrifice on and before the mercy seat. The work of an advocate suggests *conflict, argument, a presentation of facts to defend a client, the means whereby a satisfactory verdict might be obtained in a court of law.* Paul used the same word (*parakleeseos*) in 2 Corinthians 8:4 when he referred to the ardent efforts of the saints to persuade the apostle to accept a gift. The work of the advocate also implies the presence of an adversary resisting what was being said and done. John shed light on the subject when he wrote, "Now is come salvation and strength. . .*for the accuser of our brethren is cast down; which accused them before our God day and night*" (Rev. 12:10). This name, which was mentioned only once, reveals a new aspect of the amazing work of the Lord Jesus Christ.

*An advocate's prerogative. . .to accept or refuse a client*

Occasionally, an accused person decides to defend himself, to act as his own counselor, in a court of law. No one can compel him to engage an attorney, and a lawyer cannot be compelled to accept a client. There are men who refuse to plead the case of a known criminal. First, the advocate must be requested by a client to take a case, and if the lawyer chooses, he then accepts the assignment. John evidently liked the term *advocate* because it applied to his Lord. The apostle believed Jesus was the greatest counselor in existence, but he also acknowledged the necessity of asking for His assistance. John remembered how Jesus said, "Him that cometh to me, I will in no wise cast out" (John 6:37).

*An advocate's purpose. . .to plead a case before a judge*

The writer to the Hebrews said, "Wherefore, he is able also to save them to the uttermost that come unto God by him, *seeing he ever liveth to make intercession for them*" (Heb. 7:25). A lawyer insists on the honesty of his client. He states, "I cannot defend you unless you tell everything you know." There is hardly need to emphasize this in connection with the divine Attorney. He already knows all that can be known and in spite of our guilt, gladly accepts the task of representing us before the throne of God. Wise people eagerly accept His services, which are offered free to all.

*An advocate's problem . . . to resist an adversary*

It is significant that Satan is described as "the accuser of the brethren." The Bible tells how he criticized Job and thereafter was given permission to test the righteousness of the patriarch. There are flaws in every Christian, and it would not therefore be difficult for Satan to find areas in our lives to criticize. It is stimulating to know there is another one whose solicitations outweigh anything uttered against us.

*An advocate's pleasure . . . to receive the praise of his client*

Every lawyer expects payment for his service. Yet, for some special attorneys, the gratitude of a client is more valuable than a financial reward. To see an accused person leaving a courthouse free brings smiles of pleasure to the face and warmth to the soul. The Lord Jesus must be exceedingly thrilled when appreciation fills the souls of those set free by His intercessory ministry. Nothing brings joy to His heart more than the loving service rendered by a client whose defense was satisfactorily concluded. A man or woman who never shows gratitude after a case has been won would be unworthy of attention. It should be obvious to everybody that since Christians owe so much to the divine Advocate, no gift of service should be too great to return to Him. We cannot buy His favor, but we can thrill His soul!

# THE LION OF THE TRIBE OF JUDAH. . . the Root of David

(REVELATION 5:5)

This name, the Lion of the tribe of Judah, was one of the most significant names ever given to the Savior. It was given by an elder who stood before the throne of God and revealed the complexity of the nature of the Son of God. John, who was disturbed because no one had been found worthy to open the book with seven seals, was told not to weep, for the Lion of the tribe of Judah would do what was beyond the capabilities of others. Yet, when he looked for the Lion, he saw a Lamb that looked as though it had been slain. The heavenly host saw Jesus as the embodiment of strength, the greatest among the great, the Lion of the tribe of Judah. John saw Him as the Lamb slain, a victim of cruel men, the sacrifice which went without protest to the place of execution.

*The Lion-Lamb in Galilee (Mark 4:36-41)*

The disciples were bewildered when they considered their Master's action in the boat on the Sea of Galilee. Overcome by fatigue and weariness, the Lord slept through a tempest. Yet, when a disciple asked for assistance, Christ rebuked the elements and there was a great calm. Nonplussed and amazed, the astonished disciples considered the weakness and wonder of their Master. Their confusion was expressed in the question: "What manner of man is this that even the winds and the waves obey him?" The Lamb had been overcome by weariness, but the strength of the Lion stilled the storm.

*The Lion-Lamb in Gethsemane (Matt. 26:51-54)*

Terror had shattered the tranquillity of the garden-sanctuary. Invaders had entered the area and ugliness ruined beauty. Realizing their Master was being threatened by the mob, the disciples were seized with panic but, determined not to surrender without a fight, Peter hastily took out his sword. "And behold one of the disciples which were with Jesus, stretched out his hand, and drew his sword, and struck a servant of the high priest's, and smote off his ear. Then Jesus said. . . .Thinkest thou that I cannot now pray to my Father, and he shall presently give me more than twelve legions of angels?" The angels were not summoned, and the disciples watched as the Master was bound and led away. They might have been excused if they considered the event incomprehensible.

*The Lion-Lamb in the glory (Rev. 5:5)*

The book with seven seals related to the redemption of property; all Hebrews understood its significance. Witnesses had appended their names to the scroll of transaction, within which were the terms by which the land could be reclaimed. When such a person was forthcoming, he was entitled to break the seals, reveal what had to be done, and then do it. It is necessary to remember that the scene took place after the homegoing of the Church. The bride of Christ had been redeemed and transported to heaven, but the planet earth remained in bondage. John wept, not because of acute disappointment, but because he feared that the redemption of earth would not be finalized. The message given to John explained how the Lion of the tribe of Judah would accomplish that great work; the Root of David would complete what had been commenced. The Lamb made salvation possible; the Lion would make it perfect! The Lamb redeemed His people; the Lion would protect them on their pilgrimage to the Promised Land.

This conflicting aspect of the life and ministry of the Lord may be hard to comprehend, but it reveals superlative truth. It is stimulating to remember that the hands that created the universe could touch a leper; the arms which encircled eternity embraced children. The Savior was He who loved, sought, and brought us into His fold.

Precious Name, Oh, how sweet:
Hope of earth and joy of heaven.

# THE OVERCOMER

(Revelation 17:14)

This was one of the Lord's most suggestive names; it reflected not what He was, but what He accomplished. Many of the names of Jesus revealed the wonder of His work, the dignity of His office, and the majesty of His personality. That the Lord of the universe should need to overcome trials, conflicts, temptations, and hardship brings the Lord of creation down to the level of the oppressed and enables people to appreciate the message sent to the Hebrew Christians. "For we have not an high priest which cannot be touched with the feeling of our infirmities; but was in all points tempted like as we are, yet without sin" (Heb. 4:15). The Greek word used in the text means "to sympathize," and the verse should read: "We do not have a high priest who is unable to sympathize." Jesus, the Son of God, was not a stranger to temptation. It was only by constant watchfulness that He overcame the forces arrayed against Him. To discover the secret and source of His unfailing strength should be the most important aim in the life of every Christian.

*The Lord overcame by prayerfulness*

It has been well said, "If you are too busy to pray, you are too busy!" The modern world is vastly different from what it was two thousand years ago. Life in the times of Jesus was lived at a more leisurely pace. It was not too difficult for men to leave their tasks and to spend days following the Savior. One wonders what would happen if business life ceased completely in a large city were every employee to go into the country to hear an evangelist! Nevertheless, it would be difficult to find a person more active than Jesus of Nazareth. Circumstances dictated that He would be in constant demand. People sought aid before sunrise and remained throughout the day. He became so weary that He slept through a storm on the sea. The only privacy the Lord ever experienced came when "in the morning, rising up a great while before day, he went out, and departed into a solitary place, and there prayed" (Mark 1:35). During the times of fellowship with His Father, the Lord "charged His spiritual batteries" so effectively that they never lost their power throughout the day! That amazing strength enabled Him to be a continual Overcomer. Most of our defeats are the result of our being too busy to pray!

*The Lord overcame by thoughtfulness*

It is significant that when Satan tempted the Lord in the wilderness, each temptation was negated by the Savior's use of the Scripture. Jesus filled His mind with the Word of God and used the promises of the Almighty to offset every challenge of the devil. The Savior did what Paul later advised the Philippians to do. "Finally, brethren, whatsoever things are true, whatsoever things are honest, whatsoever things are just, whatsoever things are pure, whatsoever things are lovely, whatsoever things are of good report; if there be any virtue, and if there be any praise, *think on these things*" (Phil. 4:8). When Christians permit evil thoughts to remain in their minds, defeat is never far away. The Savior remembered the refreshing promises of His Father and was prepared when evil attacked Him.

*The Lord overcame by carefulness*

Jesus was extremely careful in all He said and did. His motto could have been, "Make haste slowly!" This became obvious when He refused to answer the accusers of the woman who was caught in the act of adultery. Instead of replying immediately, "He stooped down and wrote on the ground" (see John 8:1-11). It was also evident when He was asked about the legality of paying taxes to Caesar. He refrained from supplying a spontaneous answer and requested a coin (see Matt. 22:17-22). Jesus never rushed blindly into anything! He was extremely careful throughout His entire ministry and, consequently, never regretted a statement or deed. John was assured that all Christians would be able to share the triumphs of the Lord, for in describing a scene to take place at the end of time, he wrote, "The accuser of our brethren is cast down, which accused them before our God day and night. *And they overcame him* by the blood of the Lamb, and by the word of their testimony; and they loved not their lives unto the death" (Rev. 12:10-11). The Lord and His followers share their conquests; they are overcomers.

# THE KING OF KINGS AND LORD OF LORDS

(REVELATION 19:16)

The title "King of kings" is probably the most majestic and comprehensive of all the names given to Christ. Its glory and splendor extend throughout many areas. The wise men who came to Bethlehem called Jesus the "King of the Jews" (Matt. 2:2), a title possibly associated with the title "Messiah." When Nathaniel came to Jesus, he exclaimed: "Thou art the King of Israel" (John 1:49). John, describing what he saw in heaven, addressed the Lord as "thou King of saints" (Rev. 15:3). When the writer to the Hebrews compared the Lord with Melchizedek, he explained that Christ was a Priest of the same order, a royal Priest, and was "the King of peace" (Heb. 7:2). David expressed his thoughts in another way when he wrote: "Lift up ye heads, O ye gates. . . and *the King of glory* shall come in. . ." (Ps. 24:7). If Christ be the *King of Glory* and the *King of heaven* (Dan. 4:37) then He is indisputably the *King of angels* (See Heb. 1:6-8).

*The amazing acclamation. . . the King of Glory (Ps. 24:7)*

During the affliction endured by Job, God asked an important question: "Where wast thou when I laid the foundations of the earth?. . . . When the morning stars sang together, and all the sons of God shouted for joy?" (Job 38:4,7). John said of his Lord that "without him was not anything made that was made" (John 1:3). The scene described in these verses beggars description. Before time began, there was joy in the presence of the Creator-Christ when He brought worlds into being. Music resounded throughout the eternal world when the universe appeared. The Lord made rivers to flow, birds to sing, flowers to be fragrant, and the earth to be resplendent with beauty and life. When the earliest inhabitants of the created worlds saw the scintillating splendor of the Lord, they united in praising their king. He was truly *the King of Glory.*

*The awful anguish. . . the King of the Jews (Matt. 27:37)*

Throughout His ministry on earth, the Lord was often called "The King of the Jews," but the testimony was never more provocative than at Calvary. It has been written, "And sitting down they watched him there; and set up over his head his accusation written, *THIS IS JESUS THE KING OF THE JEWS.*" It seems almost incomprehensible that He who had been acclaimed by angels, should be crucified by men. It appears to be beyond imagination that He who made the forests should hang upon one of His own trees. It was never expected that He who made blood to run in the veins of men should shed His own blood for those who killed Him. The King of heaven gave Himself for unworthy people; in return, they gave Him *a crown of thorns.*

*The actual anointing . . . the King of saints (Heb. 2:9)*

A prince never becomes a king until he is crowned. The Prince of Peace could hardly become the King of saints until the official coronation had been celebrated in heaven. After the ascension of the Lord, He was "crowned with glory and honor," and became the official representative of His people at the throne of God. Jesus earned the right to be the royal representative of His people in all matters related to their faith and future. The high priest of Israel was anointed with oil on the day of ordination, but Christ was honored when God signally bestowed upon Him heaven's highest accolade. That also was an occasion when angels sang together for joy.

*The absolute affirmation . . . the King of kings (Rev. 19:16)*

God has always had a plan for this earth, and the success of His work was always assured. David wrote, "The LORD said unto my Lord, Sit thou at my right hand, until I make thine enemies thy footstool" (Ps. 110:1). The writer to the Hebrews associated that statement with the Savior, and indicated that God intended to honor the Lord before the eyes of all people (see Heb. 10:12-13). John, describing the ultimate moment of triumph, said, "And I saw heaven opened, and behold, a white horse; and he that sat upon him was called Faithful and True. . . . His name is called the Word of God . . . KING OF KINGS, and LORD OF LORDS." Christ was crowned with thorns (John 19:2), glory, and honor (Heb. 2:9) as well as with many crowns (Rev. 19:12). The first explains the secret of our happiness; the second, the reason for our help; and the third, the confidence we have in our eternal home.

# THE ALPHA AND OMEGA

(REVELATION 21:6)

This may be one of the most significant names or titles ever given to the Savior. It is important to recognize that it is mentioned four times in the Book of Revelation (1:8; 1:11; 21:6; and 22:13). The Lord possibly desired to emphasize that He was the Complete One, that nothing existed before Him, that nothing supersedes Him in time, and in every matter of eternal verity, that He will have the final word. The Bible begins with God: "In the beginning God. . . ." (Gen. 1:1) and ends with Christ: "The grace of our Lord Jesus Christ be with you all" (Rev. 22:21). All roads within the Scripture lead to the Savior.

*He is the beginning and end of creation*

When the psalmist was overwhelmed by problems and surrounded by unpleasant circumstances, he turned to God and said, "Of old hast thou laid the foundations of the earth: and the heavens are the work of thine hands. They shall perish, but thou shalt endure; yea, all of them shall wax old like a garment; as a vesture shalt thou change them, and they shall be changed; but thou art the same, and thy years shall have no end" (Ps. 102:25-27). Even the most brilliant men stand in awe when confronted by the immensity of God, who breathed life into every living thing, designed the universe, and gave careful attention even to the smallest things. When He surveyed His handiwork, He was pleased, for it was good! When this world is destroyed by fire (2 Peter 3:10-13), God will create a new heaven and earth "wherein dwelleth righteousness."

*He is the author and finisher of our faith*

The writer to the Hebrews said, "let us lay aside every weight . . . looking unto Jesus *the author and finisher of our faith*. . . ." (Heb. 12:1-2). Christians testify concerning their conversion to Christ and often describe events which led to the moment of surrender. A careful scrutiny of the Word of God reveals that we owe everything to God. He chose us before the world began (Eph. 1:4). As the Good Shepherd, He came to seek us (John 1:11), and even our faith is a gift from God. Paul said faith was a gift of the Spirit (1 Cor. 12:8-9), and emphasizing the same truth, Peter wrote "to them that have *obtained* like precious faith with us . . ." (2 Peter 1:1). True faith begins in heaven, comes to repentant people, and finally returns to the place from which it came. All we have and are, we owe to God. Christ loved us, sought us, found and saved us, and one day will make us like Himself. John said, "Beloved, now are we the sons of God, and it doth not yet appear what we shall be; but we know that, when he shall appear, we shall be like him; for we shall see him as he is'' (1 John 3:2). In the words of the hymn writer, Robert Robinson, ''Oh, to grace, how great a debtor, daily I'm constrained to be.''

*He is the Alpha and Omega of revelation*

It is thought-provoking that the name ''Alpha and Omega'' is found twice at the beginning of the Revelation and twice at its end. When the Lord spoke to John, He said, ''I am Alpha and Omega, the first and the last. . . what thou seest, write in a book, and send it unto the seven churches'' (Rev. 1:11). When John had fulfilled his commission and when the book was almost completed, the Lord repeated His earlier statement, saying, ''I am Alpha and Omega, the beginning and the end, the first and the last.'' He then said, ''For I testify unto every man that heareth the prophecy of this book; if any man shall add unto these things, God shall add unto him the plagues that are written in this book: and if any man shall take away from the words of the prophecy of this book, God shall take away his part out of the book of life, and out of the holy city, and from the things which are written in this book'' (Rev. 22:18-19). Christ was the beginning and end of the revelation God gave to men. If there is any meaning in language, then all that God had to communicate may be found within the Bible. Cults have either substituted other volumes or denied the veracity of the Scripture, but the ancient statements of God have never been invalidated. The Bible is a well from which sincere people draw refreshment to meet every need of their thirsty souls.

Breathe, Oh, breathe Thy loving Spirit
Into every troubled breast
Let us all in Thee inherit
Let us find that promised rest.
Take away our love for sinning,
Alpha and Omega be;
End of faith, as its beginning,
Set our hearts at liberty.

# THE BRIGHT AND MORNING STAR

(REVELATION 22:16)

"The ancient Hebrews knew very little of the starry heavens, and no indications are given in Scripture of scientific astronomy. We find there only observations of landmen (Amos 5:8) and especially shepherds (Ps. 8:3)" (*Unger's Bible Dictionary,* p. 1044). Nevertheless, the people of the ancient world gazed on the star-filled heavens and became aware of certain phenomena, reference to which was made in the prophetical writings.

*God's sign in the sky*

To gaze at the celestial panorama was a nightly attraction enjoyed by shepherds and travelers. They were aware of the bright light which heralded the approach of the dawn, and called it the "Morning Star" (2 Peter 1:19 and Rev. 2:28; 22:16). W. White, Jr., writing in the *Zondervan Pictorial Encyclopedia of the Bible,* says on page 397 of volume 1, "The morning star is never a star, but any one of the planets, Mercury, Venus, Mars, Jupiter and Saturn, when it is in position to be seen in the East just before sunrise. At times, two or three may be seen in the sky. However, the Bible passages most likely refer to Venus, since it is the brightest, and sometimes can be seen long after the sun is up." When other stars or planets fade into insignificance before the splendor of the dawn, the morning star seems to be at its best as it announces the termination of night and the birth of a new day. Seafarers look for it, and ancient mariners often checked their courses by its position. It always appeared to be the brightest and best of God's sentinels in the sky.

*God's Son in the Scriptures*

It is significant that the Morning Star was one of the names which Christ gave to Himself. He said, "I am the bright and morning star" (Rev. 22:16). All the early Christians recognized the appropriateness of the statement, for the appearance of the Savior proclaimed that the long, dark night of superstition was ending and that the birth of the gospel era would lead to a day which would never end. Weary and sometimes bewildered travelers charted their homeward course by it, and those who sat in the shadow of death knew help was near. The Lord indicated that every facet of truth suggested by the Morning star was being fulfilled in Him. Furthermore, this claim was made concerning His coming to Bethlehem and His return, at the end of time, to establish an everlasting kingdom. Christ reflected the glory of an eternal world, and only earth-born clouds could hide Him from the view of His servants. He was, indeed, the Bright and Morning Star.

*God's song in the soul*

Simon Peter was one of the first Christians to recognize the suggestiveness of that illustrious name. He wrote, "We have also a more sure word of prophecy whereunto ye do well that ye take heed, as unto a light that shineth in a dark place, until the day dawn, and *the day star* [ Morning Star] arise in your hearts" (2 Peter 1:19). The risen Christ sent a message to the Christians at Thyatira saying, "And he that overcometh, and keepeth my works unto the end, to him will I give power over the nations. . . . And I will give him *the morning star*" (Rev. 2:26, 28). At a later date, as recorded by John, the Lord said, "I am the bright and morning star." Peter believed that the Savior in His risen splendor would become the joy and inspiration of those who overcame for His sake. They would know, amid the crises of life, that the darkest hour always preceded the dawn. This glorious realization enabled them to sing in the darkness. The apostle evidently considered the brilliance of the Morning Star to be a wonderful radiance, emanating from the souls of those redeemed by the precious blood of Christ. Some men crouch in the gloom and see only misery, defeat, and doubt. Others look to the sky and live in the joyful anticipation of a sunrise. Probably C. W. Fry had these thoughts in mind when he wrote his famous words,

I've found a Friend in Jesus,
He's everything to me.
He's the fairest of ten thousand to my soul.
"The Lily of the Valley"
In Him alone I see
All I need to cleanse and make me fully whole.
In sorrow He's my comfort;
In trouble He's my stay.
He tells me every care on Him to roll;
He's the Lily of the Valley,
The "Bright and Morning Star;"
He's the fairest of ten thousand to my soul.

# ALPHABETICAL INDEX WITH SCRIPTURE TEXT

# BOOKS BY IVOR POWELL

## BIBLE CAMEOS
These 80 graphic "thumb-nail" sketches are brief biographies of Bible people. Pungent and thought-provoking studies.
ISBN 0-8254-3515-3 192 pp. paperback

## BIBLE GEMS
Mini-messages with an ample supply of sermon starters, illustrations and deep truths from God's Word.
ISBN 0-8254-3527-7 176 pp. paperback

## BIBLE HIGHWAYS
Scripture texts are linked together, suggesting highways through the Bible from Genesis to Revelation.
ISBN 0-8254-3521-8 176 pp. paperback

## BIBLE PINNACLES
A spiritual adventure into the lives and miracles of Bible characters and the meaningful parables of our Lord.
ISBN 0-8254-3516-1 192 pp. paperback

## BIBLE TREASURES
In refreshingly different style and presentation, these 80 Bible miracles and parables are vividly portrayed.
ISBN 0-8254-3518-8 182 pp. paperback

## BIBLE WINDOWS
Anecdotes and stories are, in fact, windows through which the Gospel light shines, to illumine lessons for preachers.
ISBN 0-8254-3522-6 180 pp. paperback

## DAVID: HIS LIFE AND TIMES
David, the "sweet Psalmist of Israel," comes alive in the unique and refreshing manner typical of Ivor Powell's writings.
ISBN 0-8254-3523-3 416 pp. paperback

## MATTHEW'S MAJESTIC GOSPEL
You will find almost everything you need in developing sermons: theme, outline, expository notes, preaching homilies.
ISBN 0-8254-3525-0 526 pp. hardback